THE ENVIRONMENT

and

BRITISH POLITICS

Duncan Watts

Series Editor: David Simpson

Hodder & Stoughton

A MEMBER OF THE HODDER HEADLINE GROUP

ACKNOWLEDGEMENTS

The publishers would like to thank the following for permission to reproduce copyright images:

ECOSCENE/W. Lawler, p 7, top; Life File/Nigel Shuttleworth, p 7, bottom; CORBIS/David H. Wells, p 48; CORBIS/Bettmann, p 94; ECOSCENE/Ian Harwood, p 105.

Orders: please contact Bookpoint Ltd, 39 Milton Park, Abingdon, Oxon OX14 4TD. Telephone: (44) 01235 400414, Fax: (44) 01235 400454. Lines are open from 9.00–6.00, Monday to Saturday, with a 24 hour message answering service. Email address: orders@bookpoint.co.uk

A catalogue record for this title is available from The British Library

ISBN 0 340 747919

First published 1999
Impression number 10   9   8   7   6   5   4   3   2   1
Year   2005   2004   2003   2002   2001   2000   1999

Cover photo from PA News.

Typeset by Transet Limited, Coventry, England.
Printed in Great Britain for Hodder & Stoughton Educational, a division of Hodder Headline plc, 338 Euston Road, London NW1 3BH by Redwood Books, Trowbridge, Wilts.

CONTENTS

PREFACE

A/AS Level syllabuses in Government and Politics aim to develop knowledge and understanding of the political system of the UK. They cover its local, national and European Union dimensions, and include comparative studies of aspects of other political systems, in order to ensure an understanding of the distinctive nature of the British political system. The minimum requirements for comparative study are aspects of systems with a separation of powers, how other systems protect the rights of individuals and how other electoral systems work.

Access to Politics is a series of concise topic books which cover the syllabus requirements, providing students with the necessary resources to complete the course successfully.

General advice on approaching exam questions

To achieve high grades you need to demonstrate consistency. Clearly address all parts of a question, make good use of essay plans or notes, and plan your time to cover all the questions.

Make your answers stand out from the crowd by using contemporary material to illustrate them. You should read a quality newspaper and listen to or watch appropriate programmes on radio and television.

Skills Advice

You should comprehend, synthesise and interpret political information in a variety of forms:

- Analyse and evaluate political institutions, processes and behaviour, political arguments and explanations.
- Identify parallels, connections, similarities and differences between aspects of the political systems studied.
- Select and organise relevant material to construct arguments and explanations leading to reasoned conclusions.
- Communicate the arguments with relevance, clarity and coherence, using vocabulary appropriate to the study of Government and Politics.

David Simpson

1

INTRODUCTION

IN THE 1950s and 1960s, the words 'environment' or 'green' were infrequently used in daily discussion, and the subject was of minor interest or concern to practising politicians in Europe or across the Atlantic. Now they are part of our everyday vocabulary, and we have become much more conscious of the threats to our accepted way of life which human-made disasters can bring about. The mercury-poisoning episode in Minamata, Japan; the leak of poisonous gas in Seveso, Italy and in Bhopal, India; and the escape of nuclear waste at Chernobyl, all helped to alert us to the danger, and prompted the formation of environmentalist movements throughout the world.

In common with the situation in other advanced Western countries, little attention was initially paid by British people to problems of the environment. Natural resources seemed to be readily available so that it was easy to assume that the supply was unlimited. The situation began to change in the 1960s, a key development being the publication in the USA of Rachel Carson's *Silent Spring*, which directed public concern to the dangers of unchecked exploitation of the environment and the harmful effects of the use of pesticides. Various reports began to document the hazards associated with pollution and over-intensive production, whilst others examined the loss of plant and animal species.

By the 1980s the British membership of groups such as Greenpeace and Friends of the Earth (FoE) had rocketed, and publishers issued new books about the environment. *The Green Consumer Guide* was an immediate best-seller and helped to promote interest in the possibilities of environmentally-conscious consumerism. Supermarkets competed to produce the most ecological forms of washing powder and sell the greatest quantity of free-range eggs. Companies were keen to parade their green credentials, and in the case of The Body Shop an entirely new business was created to reflect the increased awareness. More of us than ever before recycle our paper, sort out different colours of bottles for the bottle bank and cook additive-free tins of beans. Today many politicians claim to be green.

WHAT IS MEANT BY ENVIRONMENTALISM?

It is clear that there is today a growing appreciation of the impact which our activities have on the natural surroundings, with opposition to bypasses, motorways, airports, nuclear power stations and other human-made developments which appear to threaten the environment in some way. There are similar anxieties about the way in which we pollute the air, earth and sea, and about the way in which we kill animals for money or sport. In other words there is a growing environmental awareness, a move towards a reconciliation between humanity and nature.

Environmentalism has been defined by Allaby (*Green Facts*) as 'the physical, chemical and biotic conditions surrounding an organism'. Our concern is with the human organism and therefore the human environment. In a sense, as we all share the conditions around us, it is to our common advantage to show an interest in the environment, for these conditions are basic to our survival. Hence few would say that they are anti-environmentalists.

At this point a distinction may be made between environmentalists and ecologists:

- **Environmentalists** are committed to protection of the environment and see the importance of ensuring that human beings meet their obligations to cherish the air, sea and land, and all the life forms that inhabit them. However, they do not necessarily claim that all species of life have the same rights, and their approach is essentially human-centred; they want us to protect nature, but ultimately this is for reasons of benefit to men and women.
- **Ecologists** go further and stress the inter-connectedness of all forms of life. They do not see people as being endowed with superior wisdom or with greater rights, and wish to see all species treated equally.

In voicing their concerns, moderate environmentalists and more radical ecologists are to be found in new kinds of political movements. Both in their goals and in the means they employ to achieve them, they are distinct from followers of earlier ideas and of the organisations set up to mobilise support for them. Younger, better-informed sections of society have been interested in adopting novel political strategies such as demonstrations, protests, sit-ins and passive resistance. Like those engaged in the campaigns for women's rights, international peace and Third World politics, they are more interested in being actively involved.

In the past, political leaders set the political agenda from above, but in the 'new politics' the impetus comes from below, for adherents aim at mass participation and self-direction. In the 'old politics', leadership came from the narrow ruling elite, but in the 'new politics', pressure is placed upon those who dominate the existing structures of power. In furtherance of their aims, subscribers to the 'new politics' adopt modes of organisation which are less formal and hierarchical, and a characteristic of these newer social movements is that they often take the form of loose networks of individuals and groups which meet to advance their cause and plan their campaigns.

HISTORY

New social movements are, as their name implies, a recent phenomenon. However, there has been concern about the environment for a much longer period than the last 30 years, but whereas primitive people sensed that humanity and its surroundings were indivisible, modern people have had to relearn that lesson. According to Lowe and Goyder (*Environmental Groups in Britain*) there have been four eras in environmental activity over the last 100 years:

1 At the end of the nineteenth century there was an upsurge in the growth of organisations such as the Royal Society for the Prevention of Cruelty to Animals (RSPCA), National Trust and Garden Cities Association (later the Town and Country Planning Association) which were all concerned with the quality of life and the desire to preserve its best features. These were conservation bodies interested in preserving the countryside, its inhabitants and fine buildings.

2 The interwar era saw the emergence of organisations more concerned to encourage people to benefit from what the countryside could offer them in a pre-television age – eg the Ramblers' Association, Pedestrians' Association and Council for the Preservation of Rural England.

3 The late 1950s was an era in which groups were developed which sought to preserve the best of the past and avoid the horrors of modern life by organising such movements as the Civic Trust, Victorian Society and Noise Abatement Society.

4 The early 1970s saw the formation of many new groups such as FoE, Greenpeace, Save Britain's Heritage, Transport 2000 and a whole host of local amenity organisations of which many were affiliated to the Civic Trust.

To the Victorians the enemy was the private landowner who was pre-occupied with his own self-interest at the expense of the community. Part of the answer lay in governmental action. Today governments are seen as part of the problem in that the policies they put forward – be they programmes for motorway development, extending airports or privatising public utilities – can be detrimental to the environment. Yet there is a common thread which runs through all the periods we have mentioned. This is that individuals involved in each movement have advocated that we should be less concerned with the accumulation of greater wealth and increasing the standard of living, and more concerned with other values.

Environmental concerns cover several areas and spring from various motives, ranging from the noble to the less noble. Some people are primarily concerned with the better use of resources and the protection of the community. Others are more concerned with retaining the beauty of their own part of the environment by staving off development, so that for some environmentalists the Nimby syndrome (*not in my backyard*) is a factor in their thinking. Nimbies don't mind development as such but do not wish it to impact upon their own lives. Thus in the past many of those in the Council for the Protection (formerly Preservation) of Rural England (CPRE) have been more concerned to preserve the rural way of life from which they themselves benefit, than about the lifestyle of those who inhabit overcrowded cities. Environmentalism can therefore embrace social concern and simple selfish interest.

We have therefore two conflicting threads running through the thinking of those who express environmental awareness:

1   For the most genuinely committed there is the perspective which says that human values have become too materialistic, and which stresses the importance of the quality of life rather than the endless search for material progress. From this perspective it may be more important to save the countryside so that everyone can benefit from the wildlife being left undisturbed, than to build a bypass which may alleviate traffic problems for a while, but in so doing mean that more pollution is pumped into the atmosphere.
2   Others take the view that change is not to be embraced, because development means a disruption to the even tenor of some people's comfortable lives, and this is a case of the few wishing to preserve themselves from the impact of the many who might use their facilities and ruin their outlook.

Because of this self-interested aspect, environmentalists are sometimes charged with elitism. Certainly much environmentalism is a rural phenomenon, so that the minority of people who live in rural areas do not often concern themselves with the many more who live in urban ones. This was recognised by a Labour politician of the last generation who became secretary of state for the environment, Anthony Crosland. He used to complain that members of the environmental lobby were:

hostile to growth and indifferent to the needs of ordinary people...people who had themselves secured the good life and were actively engaged in seeking to deny others the change to share in its blessings.

Yet more recently, environmentalism has been much less of a rural phenomenon, and many recent anxieties are about life in more populated areas; hence the worry about lead in petrol which gave rise to a successful clamour for a change in

public policy. Similarly many examples of protest against motorway development have taken place in urban areas. Moreover much environmentalism has been preoccupied with conditions worldwide such as the behaviour of multinational companies (eg Shell BP and the impact of its pipeline in Nigeria).

PRESENT-DAY ANXIETIES

Ever since the Industrial Revolution the idea of human progress in Britain has been associated with industrial development. Before this the economy was primarily agricultural, and the lifestyle adopted by the bulk of the population posed no threat to the environment which it was in their interests to conserve and protect. In the era since the Industrial Revolution, good husbandry of the country's natural resources gave way to exploitation as industrialists sought new sources of raw materials as cheaply as possible. The period has been characterised by ever-increasing production and the provision of a vast range of goods and services, and in the process the material standard of living of most people has improved out of all recognition. But this has been at a cost, and over the last generation environmentalists have emerged to tell us that the unrestrained use of our resources cannot continue. They argue that the environment has been the unacknowledged source of our material prosperity but that we have made too many demands upon it. They have called for a reassessment of our national and global priorities.

A post-materialistic philosophy emerged in a publication by a group of economists, industrialists and scientists who met together in a think-tank known as the Club of Rome. Their report, *The Limits to Growth*, predicted ecological disaster if economic growth was not controlled. More specifically it suggested that:

- Given current population growth, industrialisation, pollution and resource depletion, the limits to growth on this planet would be attained within 100 years. It was claimed that industrial capacity would sharply decline and that some raw materials would soon be used up. Aluminium supplies would be exhausted within 31 years (2001) and copper might run out even before then.
- It is possible to create environmental and economic stability which could be sustained in the long term, but that the need to tackle the problem was urgent and should be undertaken as soon as possible.

A second Club of Rome report published two years later, *Mankind at the Turning Point*, was more concerned with the Third World. The argument advanced was that production of raw materials would suffer from acute resource shortages which would spread to the world's economy and paralyse it. This document received less publicity, but the work of the Club of Rome became something of a rallying point for the ecology movement.

The pursuit of economic growth was and is seen as intrinsic to environmental problems, although much of the more recent concern has been concerned with pollution. One theory is that rapid population increase has caused pollution, but most pollution occurs in the more developed world where population growth has been checked. Therefore the idea has developed that as societies become increasingly affluent so too they consume more goods, and that it is increased production which causes the spread of pollution and consequent damage to the environment. The development of new technologies on which many consumer societies depend has been a factor, for the increased use of products which will not degrade biologically (eg detergents and plastic) has led to environmental problems. So too has intensive farming, made possible by the use of various chemical fertilisers.

GLOBAL SUSTAINABLE DEVELOPMENT

'Sustainability' is a term used by environmentalists who want to see an alternative to economic growth. The phrase is widely supported by international non-governmental organisations, particularly those active in shaping the global environmental agenda. Its heritage is traceable to the publication of the 1987 Report of the World Commission on Environment and Development (popularly known as the Brundtland Commission). Entitled *Our Common Future*, the document concludes that the world cannot sustain the growth required to meet the needs and aspirations of the world's projected population unless it develops radically different approaches to basic issues of economic expansion, equity, resource management, energy efficiency and the like. It defined a sustainable society as one that 'meets the needs of the present without compromising the ability of future generations to meet their own needs'.

The Brundtland Report was an important landmark in the rapid emergence of environmental issues as global concerns, but there have been others before and since. We have already referred to *The Limits to Growth* analysis, and in the same year in which it was produced, a United Nations Conference on the Human Environment (the Stockholm Conference) drew attention to the fact that:

In the developing countries, most of the environmental problems are caused by under-development … In the industrialised countries, environmental problems are generally related to industrialisation and technological development.

It urged the need for governments of the more developed nations to take action to lessen the gap between themselves and what used to be called the Third World countries, in order to assist in their sustainable development. Since then, there have been many conferences on this and a range of other environmental topics, with scores of environmental treaties negotiated and new international agencies put into place to promote cooperation and monitor environmental developments.

REMOVING THE RAINFOREST

VICTIMS OF POLLUTION FALL-OUT

This increase in global environmental consciousness reached its peak with the Earth Summit, held in Rio de Janeiro to mark the twentieth anniversary of the Stockholm Conference. Its programme of action, *Agenda 21*, embodied the need for political commitment to a broad range of environmental and development goals. Whereas the environment and development had sometimes been treated previously as conflicting areas of policy – with development imperilling and degrading the environment – the concept of sustainability was used to galvanise a simultaneous treatment of both. Since the Rio gathering, countless books and articles have asked how and whether the ambitious goals can be achieved, a common thread being the belief that sustainability cannot be realised without dramatic changes in the economic, social and political fabric of the world as we know it. As Mahatma Gandhi remarked a half century ago:

The world has enough for everyone's need, but not for everyone's greed.

ENVIRONMENTALISM TODAY

The term 'environment' covers a whole complex of questions which in one way or another affect the quality of life. For some people it means the slum in which they live or the nearby slag heap. For others it means better control over pollution or conservation of the world's finite resources. Among the variety of green concerns might be included issues ranging from the greenhouse effect, acid rain and the depletion of the ozone layer on the one hand, to dirty drinking water, unclean beaches and the killing of seals and whales on the other. All of these and many more matters come under the environmental umbrella, and different activists place greater emphasis upon campaigning against pesticides, the siting of a bypass or the export of live animals to the continent, according to their personal preference.

Organisations involved in green campaigning concentrate on one or more of these issues, and there is a substantial overlap between the membership of some of them. Activists who have campaigned against the Newbury bypass are in many cases the sort of people who might also have been worried about the treatment of animals and the use of nuclear power. Whereas some people seek redress for specific concerns which trouble them, others have a broader perspective and see all of the matters to which we have alluded as being part of a wider question. Their analysis is more fundamental and radical in its implications for society.

As the concerns and ideas of greens have become better known (see Table 1 overleaf) they have won increasing respect across the political spectrum. Indeed all the major parties have hastened to don their green wellingtons, issuing stirring policy statements about how they will protect the environment, 'green' the British economy and so forth. To some extent we are all green now.

Table 1: *Some issues of public concern*				
% WORRIED	1986	1989	1993	1996
Exhaust fumes and smog	23	33	40	41
Traffic congestion	–	–	35	42
Noise	10	13	16	15
Loss of green belt	26	27	35	38

SOURCE: THE DEPARTMENT OF THE ENVIRONMENT AND (FOR 1996) ADAPTED FROM *SOCIAL TRENDS*

Random enquiries as to what constituted green concerns and policies would probably elicit something resembling the table below:

Table 2: *Green concerns and policies*	
• Greenhouse effect	• Dogs fouling pavements
• Ozone-layer depletion	• Chemicals in food
• Dangers of nuclear power	• Use of pesticides
• Acid rain	• Green policies
• Oil slicks	• International agreements to reduce pollution and impose controls
• Seals and whales dying out	
• Dirty beaches	• Domestic legislation to tighten controls
• Litter	• Legislation/action in areas such as organic farming and consumer choice

These are the prominent issues we popularly associate with organisations like Greenpeace, FoE and individuals like Jonathon Porritt, Sara Parkin, not to mention the allegedly extraterrestrial David Icke who has claimed to be the Son of God. However, an important distinction now needs to be made. To committed members of the green movement these measures usually represent palliatives, petty reforms which are necessary but nowhere near enough. The green perspective starts elsewhere and is characterised by a more fundamental analysis: ecological rather than environmentalist; dark green rather than light green; revolutionary rather than reformist. Indeed the ecological critique and prescription is the most revolutionary philosophy since Marxism, concerned not so much with inequality as with the survival of the human race itself.

A WANING OF INTEREST? THE COUNTER-ATTACK

The greens began with small groups and local parties, and from these have developed larger movements. In some countries the parties are politically significant, elsewhere less so, but the environmental movements as a whole have been an important factor in world politics, and environmental ideas have made a significant impact in influencing other parties on the political spectrum.

However, since the high peak of the late 1980s there appears to have been a waning in support for environmental issues. In part this reflects a relegation of environmental concerns on national political agendas as more traditional political, economic and social issues have come to the fore. Moreover as we have seen in some countries, greening of the mainstream parties has occurred as they have sought to come to terms with the vote-winning potential of green parties by adopting diluted environmentalist policies themselves. In other words the need for distinctive parties to argue for green issues has been reduced.

The response within green parties has been to reassess the direction of policy and the strategies they adopt, often leading them to focus on other political issues in order to broaden their appeal. Such parties have had to think carefully about what it means to be green, and how to operate in political systems which are often unfavourable to new entrants as they struggle for recognition. Whatever the difficulties, most countries in Europe and many elsewhere now have green parties, and some have green MPs and local councillors.

THE BACKLASH

The modern environmentalist movement is more than a generation old, but although it has survived and achieved considerable influence, it now finds itself subjected to something of a backlash. Its ideas and personalities are targeted by those groups which feel threatened (including some corporations) and by right-wing political ideologues who dislike the interventionist tone of much environmentalist language. Rightwing think-tanks have long questioned the insistence on regulation as a solution to environmental problems, seeing it both as a denial of liberty and as an unnecessarily burdensome cost to business.

The Washington-based Competitive Enterprise Institute, which has support in Europe, Africa, Australia, Japan and North and Latin America, seeks to uphold the virtues of free enterprise. It works alongside another movement, Wise Use, a coalition of ranchers, miners, loggers, farmers, fishermen and fisherwomen, hunters, off-road vehicle users, property-rights advocates, industry associations, rightwing activists and corporate front groups, and has the goal of eradicating the environmental movement and its influence. It also wishes to open up national parks and wilderness areas for oil, gas and mining exploitation, and indiscriminate felling of old-growth forests so that there is unrestricted and unregulated access to terrestrial and marine resources.

It was the greens' very success in securing environmental protection legislation that forced businesses to act. Business people have responded by funding think-tanks, forming corporate front groups and pouring money into public relations in order to orchestrate an environmental backlash. The tactics employed have been to co-opt some of the language of the environmentalists on the one hand, and to demonise and marginalise adherents of the movement on the other.

Businesses began by adopting the language of environmentalists and promoting their goods in environment-friendly language so that aerosols were 'ozone-friendly', washing powders 'phosphate-free' and aluminium cans 'recyclable'. In addition marketing people have even taken over the term 'sustainable development' in order to promote a business-as-usual scenario, and the term now enjoys a broad range of support across the political spectrum.

Otherwise the tactic is to cast doubt on some environmentalist preoccupations such as global warming and the greenhouse effect on which there are many sceptics, and to use the dissent about these theories to discredit the movement as a whole. There is said to be a lack of scientific rigour in the environmentalists' case. Moreover the behaviour of many activists who seek to advance green notions comes in for special criticism. Indeed Wise Use is prepared to resort to strong language in order to cast greens into disrepute. They are labelled as Nazis, communists or fascists whose agenda is really a totalitarian one-world government. PR companies tend to urge the use of language such as 'terrorists' and 'extremists'.

Governments have sometimes joined in the denunciation, so that the Nigerian junta called Ken Saro-Wiwa a terrorist for his non-violent campaign against Shell, and anti-logging activists in Canada have been denounced as traitors and terrorists. In Britain too such language can be used by those in office. It was in 1995 that Tim Eggar, an energy minister, accused Greenpeace of 'environmental terrorism' which posed a 'threat to democracy', its campaigns being part of the new era of single-issue 'anarchy'. Anti-roads campaigners have also come in for abuse, labelled as fascists and terrorists by some spokespersons.

Once so scapegoated, such protesters are then fair game for surveillance and harassment. It is something of an irony that non-violent activists such as Saro-Wiwa became a victim of violence, and others too have reported instances of intimidation against them. *The Guardian* reported on the murder of a prominent anti-logging activist in the Solomon Islands in the same month that Saro-Wiwa was put to death, and an environmental community leader was shot by a hired killer in Latin America as he organised to preserve the rainforests on the continent.

Legal action can also follow. Strategic Lawsuits Against Public Participation (SLAPPS) have been used frequently in North America and have now spread to Australia, Asia and parts of Europe. In Britain we have had legal action against anti-roads protestors at Twyford and M11 sites. Provisions in the Criminal Justice and Public Order Act are effectively the ultimate SLAPPS because – as Rowell points out – 'they penalise intent, rather than action'.

THE CAUSE SURVIVES AND FLOURISHES

The warnings given by thousands of individuals and groups of serious hazards ahead, may sometimes be exaggerated and on occasion prove to be ill-founded. Catastrophists' arguments that a growing world population will sooner use or burn up the resources needed for survival are not new. Francis Bacon in the seventeenth century and Thomas Malthus in the eighteenth came to much the same conclusion. We are still here. Similarly there are today doom-laden allegations that we have already lost the battle to feed humanity. Alarmist claims of global catastrophe may be overstated, and on issues such as Shell's Brent Spar oil rig the case initially presented proved to be ill-informed.

The doubters are numerous, but in spite of increased scepticism about environmentalist claims, the movements continue to grow and engage tens of millions of people across the world. India possesses the largest environmentalist movement on earth, and in countries from Brazil to Mexico, Nigeria to South Africa and in scores of other southern countries, there is a flourishing movement which has in some cases inspired and guided environmentalist crusades in the north.

Any hyperbole and distortion of the facts is not the reason for sweeping fears to one side. The central message of the environmentalist lobby is not so easily dismissed, and there is an urgency in tackling several of the problems raised in this Introduction, most recently stated by the writers of the *Living Planet* report (produced in October 1998) which documented the acceleration in environmental destruction over the past generation. Reformists believe that they can be tackled individually, but for others the population can only be saved by a total transformation of human society. This is the ecological standpoint.

Ecology is concerned with the study of how living things interact and live together in a given environment, but the movements to which we refer are not ones made up of biologists, though some may be involved. They comprise informed, aware people who believe that the ideas of ecology have profound social and political implications for how people live and think.

In this book our primary concern is with the concept of eco-politics, the intersection of ecology and politics. Ecological movements deal with the impact of human activity on the environment. Politics is concerned with the exercise of power. Eco-politics, then, centres on how the various political factors influence perceptions of, and responses to, their environments. Our purpose is to explore the reactions of people and their politicians to the local, national and global environmental challenges which confront us.

SUMMARY: LANDMARKS

- 1960 Rachel Carson's *Silent Spring*.
- 1972 The Stockholm Conference, *The Limits to Growth*.
- 1987 The Brundtland Commission, *Our Common Future*.
- 1992 Rio Conference, referred to as the Earth Summit.
- 1998 The *Living Planet* report.

Revision Hints

The purpose in this Introduction has been to introduce students to many of the environmental problems which concern those involved in green movements. It is useful to have a background knowledge of the dangers posed by the pursuit of unlimited economic growth, although there is no need for detail in examinations concerned with government and politics – as opposed to those dealing with environmental science. What is desirable is to be aware of the meaning of key terms, on some of which there will be an elaboration in future chapters. It may be useful to write down the main periods in the growth of environmental concern in the nineteenth and twentieth centuries. The summary above will serve as a reminder of the key developments of the last generation. For those who wish to read more about some of the environmental problems mentioned, the Carson book and the Club of Rome and *Living Planet* reports may be of interest.

Glossary

Eco-politics   The coming together of the worlds of ecology and politics.
Eco-system   A system involving the interactions between a community and its non-living environment.
Ecologist   A person who stresses the interconnectedness of all forms of life and does not see human beings as being endowed with superior wisdom or with greater rights than other species.

Ecology   The study of the relationships between living organisms and their environment.

Environment   The external surroundings in which human beings, animals and plants live, and which affect their behaviour and development.

Environmentalist   A person concerned with the issues which affect the environment and ecology.

Green   A person who is concerned about environmental and ecological issues.

Nimby   Not in my backyard.

Sustainable development   Development capable of being maintained at a steady level without exhausting natural resources or causing severe ecological damage.

2

GREEN POLITICAL THOUGHT

Introduction

AT FIRST SIGHT, environmentalism may not seem to be a political theory or ideology at all. Many would see the environmental movement as engaged in some kind of moral crusade for better surroundings, rather than advancing a world-view such as that associated with liberalism or socialism. The environment may seem to be too narrow a cause and to lack the contentious features that are associated with creeds such as Marxism. After all, the ideas represented are surely unexceptionable, for everybody must favour a world in which we can breathe fresh air, swim in unpolluted waters and enjoy a wide array of forms of wildlife.

Yet this is not the case. Environmentalism can certainly be classified as both theory and ideology for it fulfils the characteristics of such categories as described below. Indeed arguably it is not just an ideology but the only new ideological creation of the twentieth century. Its tenets represent a challenge to traditional Western thinking, and adherents advocate ideas which run counter to the assumptions which have underlain the thought of conservatives, radicals and socialists of all varieties for two or three centuries.

In four ways environmentalism may seem to be distinctive, namely in that it:

1 Challenges accepted ideas about economic growth and human progress.
2 Denies the desirability or necessity of human beings overcoming nature as a means of social advance.
3 Does not fit comfortably into a Left–Right spectrum and indeed draws upon several strands of existing thinking.
4 Poses a different moral standpoint from which to judge human activities.

Key Points

As you read this chapter ask yourself:

- What are the main differences between environmentalism and ecology?
- How do greens of all shades view humanity's approach to nature?
- In a political sense can red and green, and blue and green mix?
- Why might a feminist be green?
- Is ecology sufficiently distinctive to be labelled an ideology in its own right?

WHAT IS A POLITICAL THEORY OR IDEOLOGY?

Political theories or philosophies are idea systems or propositions which provide an explanation of empirical data. Their prime concern is understanding and persuasion. They are not to be judged by their success in translating ideas into reality for they are not distinguished by an overt drive for power. Thus theories are not associated with a series of plans for doing, changing or mobilising. They rise above the heat of battle and concentrate on a longer perspective.

Ideology operates at different levels. It goes beyond intellectual systems and propositions. It offers a set of ideas that provides the basis for organised political action whether it be designed to retain, amend or abolish the existing system of power relationships in society. Ideologies are ideas in pursuit of realisation, and they fail in their declared purpose if there is no attempt to put them into practice. They have a job to do whereas political theories have a more tentative, unfinished character, and the debate on them is never closed. In an ideology the ideas derive from the world of philosophy but the practice pertains to the world of politics. Karl Marx caught the distinction between theory and ideology in his remark that: 'The philosophers have only interpreted the world in various ways: the point is to change it.'

As Heywood explains:

> *When we look at the world we are also engaged in imposing meaning upon it ... Our presuppositions and assumptions are rooted in broad political creeds or traditions that are usually termed 'political ideologies'. Each of these 'isms' constitutes a distinctive intellectual framework or paradigm, and each offers its own account of political reality, its own world view.*

He goes on to suggest three features which distinguish ideologies:

1 They offer an account of the existing order, usually in the form of a world-view.
2 They provide a model of a desired future, a vision of the good society.
3 They outline how political change can and should be brought about.

ENVIRONMENTAL AWARENESS: HUMANITY AND NATURE

Environmental concern is not a new phenomenon, and the origins of a green approach can be traced to the nineteenth century in which some prominent thinkers expressed their concerns about the advance of industrialism, and others sought to preserve species of wildlife and beautiful buildings. However, the combined impact of a number of changes in the natural environment have over the last generation inspired many philosophers and writers to rethink our relationship with the planet, and the species which inhabit it.

Some problems of the mid-late twentieth century such as smog and river pollution were localised in their impact, and could be dealt with by local responses. Others were more fundamental and global in their effect. These include some of the issues encountered in the Introduction such as the greenhouse effect and global warming, depletion of the ozone layer, deforestation, over-population, nuclear contamination and many more. The combined effect of such hazards was enormous, and seemed to suggest the need for a recasting of the relationship between people and their natural environment. It seemed as though human activities were assaulting the very foundations of life as we know it, and without such a pause for reflection about existing behaviour and values the planet was in a truly dire state. The vision of earth as a bottomless cornucopia of plenty, capable of resisting human designs and infinitely renewable, was in need of some revision.

In the face of global threats of the type mentioned, adherents of most ideologies seek to achieve mastery over nature and to subdue it for their own purposes, whereas environmentalists and ecologists are uneasy about any human-centred (anthropocentric) premises. The exhortation contained in the *Book of Genesis* implied an attempt to subdue nature:

> *Be fruitful, and multiply, replenish the earth, and subdue it: and have dominion over the fish of the sea, and over the fowl of the air, and over every living thing that moveth upon the earth.*
>
> *Genesis 1.28*

Today the view that humanity is the pinnacle of nature and has a responsibility to dominate and overcome it is under challenge. Rather than taking such an instrumental and totally human-centred view, ecologists proclaim an eco-centric stance which says that it is an arrogant form of speciesism to suggest that we have the right to be in control. We need a new earth-centred ethic which accepts that all life is interconnected and that all life-forms – from the smallest insect to the largest mammal, from organisms floating in the sea to plants growing in the wild, from rivers to inanimate rocks – need to be respected. They must not be treated as though they are at the disposal of human beings to damage and exploit for their own requirements. In other words nature needs to be nurtured, preserved and protected for its own sake, not just out of a concern for our own interests.

The green attitude to our place in nature echoes a long tradition, its origins dating back to ancient philosophies in China, India and elsewhere. Primitive societies recognised that people and the environment were indivisible. Their attitude concerning the need for harmony with nature was restated in a famous response made in 1855 by a Red Indian, Chief Seattle, to the demand of the US government for rights of purchase over some established Indian territory. The passage has been oft-quoted by environmentalists as they seek to portray us as part of, rather than master of, nature:

> *How can you buy or sell the sky? We do not own the freshness of the air or the sparkle of the water. How then can you buy them from us? Every part of the earth is sacred to my people, holy in their memory and experience. We know that the white man does not understand our ways. He is a stranger who comes in the night, and takes from the land whatever he needs. The Earth is not his friend but his enemy, and when he's conquered it, he moves on. He kidnaps the earth from his children. His appetite will devour the Earth, and leave behind a desert. If all the beasts were gone we would die from a great loneliness of the spirit, for whatever happens to the beasts happens also to us. All things are connected. Whatever befalls the Earth, befalls the children of the Earth.*

Ashby (*Reconciling Man with the Environment*) argues that having been encouraged via Judaeo-Christian beliefs to dominate and exploit its surroundings, modern society has seemingly rediscovered the old truths. We have done so not by the intuition of our predecessors but through the evidence of science. Greens are in the forefront of this back-to-nature approach.

SHADES OF GREEN THINKING

Within the orbit of green thinking, there are several different strands as represented by individuals and competing groups. There is a continuum ranging from moderates to radicals, and the differences between the two polar positions range from disagreements over essential questions of substance to conflict over issues of strategy and tactics.

MODERATES AND RADICALS
(LIGHT/SHALLOW V DARK/DEEP GREENS)

In the view of conservationists and moderate environmentalists, the good life is not radically different from the one we presently lead. Radical environmentalists or ecologists have a distinctive vision, and Dobson sees this as the reason for arguing that 'ecologism can properly take its place alongside other political ideologies'. Ecologism has things to say about the whole range of political, social and economic life. Environmentalism is green with a small g whereas Green, as in Green politics, has a large one, 'for the deep Green presents a challenge to the political social, economic and scientific consensus that dominates the late twentieth century'. Deep greens are not concerned to reform society's present direction, for this reinforces values associated with affluence and technology. They call them into question, and see themselves as making a challenge to society in the wake of failed industrial system.

Porritt and Winner (*The Coming of the Greens*) express the perspective of the ecologist:

> *The most radical [Green aim] seeks nothing less than a non-violent revolution to overthrow our whole polluting, plundering and materialistic industrial society and, in its place, to create a new economic and social order which will allow human beings to live in harmony with the planet. In those terms, the Green Movement lays claim to being the most radical and important political and cultural force since the birth of socialism.*

The Porritt view as expressed in *Seeing Green* is that 'ecologism is not environmentalism':

> *It seems quite clear that whereas a concern for the environment is an essential part of being green, it is … by no means the same thing as being green.*

Radicals or ecologists insist that care for the environment presupposes a radical change in our relationship to it and in the whole mode of our economic, political and social life. Whereas moderates want an approach which manages problems, secure in the belief that they can be solved without fundamental changes in present values or patterns of production and consumption, ecologists think differently. Their developed sense of the good life is different in important and fundamental respects from other ideologies. Ecologism seeks radically to question a whole series of existing practices in a way that environmentalism does not. It envisages a post-industrial future distinct from what we now know, and opposes the whole idea that our future should revolve around high growth, high-technology-expanding services, and greater leisure and self-indulgence.

LIGHT AND DARK GREENS

We might therefore distinguish between light and dark, shallow and deep greens:

- **Light green** is used to describe many people who have taken on board an amount of green thinking, and wish to see society show more concern for the way in which we treat our world. They think that many things should be conserved, and want to see an improvement in urban areas; a system of public transport which caters effectively for the needs of individuals and makes the use of the car less necessary; and a general preservation of the countryside, landscape, wildlife and buildings of architectural interest. These people want to see changes to impose controls on the destruction of our heritage which they see going on all around them. Such a programme is essentially remedial, designed to tackle specific problems.

- **Dark greens** have an extra, fundamentalist perspective which is more ecological than environmentalist. Whilst welcoming and indeed campaigning for many measures which might alleviate particular problems and eliminate certain harmful behaviour, they see these as being essentially palliatives, a holding operation pending the introduction of a different way of life. They take a longer perspective and might be inclined to point out that, for instance, the human race has been on the earth for just 2 million years or so, and spiders for some 400 million, whilst the 'civilised' world has been around for only 10,000 years. In other words, we need to have a due respect for the landscape and other forms of life which long predate us. We are but a part of the interdependent ecosystems which make up planet earth.

ECOLOGISM: DEEP-GREEN THOUGHT

As we have seen, Ashby argued that from early biblical times humans have been encouraged to see themselves as superior to other living things, and this has distanced them from their environment. It is only in the face of today's scientific evidence that we are once again beginning to identify ourselves with its protection.

Dark greens would go on to make the point that in the time of our stewardship of the earth's resources we have done infinite damage to the environment, and that over the period of industrialisation in the last 200 years appalling harm has been inflicted. We have used more than our needs for our own sustenance, and have been reckless and extravagant in the squandering of precious resources. Such failure to husband them adequately will imperil future generations. The answer according to this diagnosis lies in some limits to economic growth.

In their book, *The Limits to Growth*, Meadows, Randers and Behrens pointed to the danger of unchecked usage of resources, and advanced a series of predictions. In their view there will continue to be rapid population growth, widespread malnutrition in the undeveloped countries, and a deteriorating environment for everyone. They make the point that the USA has used up more minerals and fossil fuels in the twentieth century than all other peoples of the world throughout human history. Faced with such destruction the world has only one or two centuries left unless it can seriously address the problems of insufficient resources, shortage of arable land, and rising pollution.

According to this alarmist viewpoint, growth is central to the issue. Modern societies have become addicted to the notion of economic growth and rising living standards, both of which are associated with the purchase and consumption of ever more products harmful to the environment. Political parties promise more growth as a way of meeting the public demand for increased consumption. To the radical environmentalist a reversal of these priorities is essential. They wish to see policies which are in harmony with nature, based on more spiritual (ie non-material) values, more concerned with cooperation than competition, and concerned to ensure a genuine appreciation of what really matters in life. They want everyone to have enough to live a fulfilled lifestyle, and therefore they are not concerned with promoting a society in which the strong dominate the weak, as everyone seeks to maximise their personal wealth and possessions. They do not wish to see high income-differentials and would prefer a society in which all have enough.

Pervading their analysis is the awareness that we are but part of nature. Whereas many people see nature as existing to serve our purposes so that we are entitled to exploit whatever resources we can find, dark or deep greens see it differently. They oppose the view that the human species is at the apex of the pyramid of life. They pose an alternative vision, the same one that inspired Chief Seattle; namely that there is a oneness in creation, and humanity should respect its surroundings and fellow-inhabitants for they are of intrinsic value and beauty, entitled to their existence without our interference.

Porritt argues that the existing spectrum of political ideas from Left to Right is irrelevant because all the major political ideologies are based on the advance of industrialism and economic growth. They all agree that the way to solve the problems of society is to increase the size of the economic cake. Porritt condemns this approach and sees the conventional ideologies as representing the greatest threat to the future of humanity. He argues for a new approach based upon ecological ideas, and the vision he sets out in *Seeing Green* provides for, among other things:

- ecology
- harmony with nature
- cooperative communitarian societies
- spiritual non-material values
- sustainability and quality of life
- low income-differentials
- decentralisation and direct democracy.

Porritt's ecological approach is based upon a number of basic principles which Adams has summarised as:

SPIRITUAL AWARENESS

This embodies a love of nature and its beauty which in some ecologists achieves a mystical or quasi-religious quality, and which forms the 'spaceship earth' concept summed up well in the quotation below by Ward and Dubois (*The Care and Maintenance of a Small Planet*):

> *Today in human society, we can perhaps hope to survive in all our prized diversity provided we can achieve an ultimate loyalty to our single, beautiful and vulnerable Planet Earth. Alone in space, alone in its life supporting systems, powered by inconceivable energies ... is this not a precious home for all us earthlings? Is this not worth our love? Does it not deserve all the inventiveness and courage to preserve it from degradation and destruction and by doing so to secure our own survival?*

BIOCENTRISM / ECOCENTRISM

These principles are the opposite of that anthropocentrism which holds that humanity is at the apex of the pyramid of life and that the rest of nature is here for us to use – an attitude which justifies the exploitation of the earth and the use of animals for food and laboratory experiments. Biocentrism argues that the non-human world has intrinsic value; we should have reverence for all life and for the earth which is the source of life as well as something of great beauty.

THE SELF-SUSTAINING SOCIETY

This entails the idea that we should be happy with enough; we should not constantly want more or look to other things to gain our satisfactions. Porritt argues that a self-sustaining society is possible if we reduce consumption and unnecessary travel, control population, are selective in our use of technology (some kinds of technology are beneficial – for example, computer technology potentially enables people to work in their own homes rather than travel) and shun those forms which are wasteful and unnecessary, such as the use of private motorcars and nuclear energy.

A REDEFINED CONCEPT OF WORK

According to this principle all receive a guaranteed basic income which will enable them to survive but will not exclude extra rewards for those who wish to work more than the average. Greens do not favour mechanised agriculture but urge a return to manual labour which entails a physical involvement of men and women with the earth.

SELF-RELIANCE

This is defined by the idea that communities should be self-sufficient and hence self-reliant. Sale (*The Ecologist*, vol. 14) has produced the concept of bioregionalism, the idea that every region has the capacity to support a certain number of people on a self-sufficient basis. He also argued that people should live in smaller communities.

EQUALITY, DEMOCRACY AND DECENTRALISATION

Porritt urges that the characteristics of nature should determine political and social forms. In order to respond to the diversity of nature we should embrace attitudes such as toleration, democracy and decentralisation. He and other greens favour small, self-contained, self-governing communities attached to each locality, with inhabitants enjoying a democratic sharing and peaceful life, at one with nature and respectful of other life forms. Such a vision is akin to the anarchic communes advocated by thinkers like Mikhail Bakunin and William Morris in the nineteenth century.

GREEN THINKING: ITS PLACE ON THE POLITICAL SPECTRUM

Green political thinking has sometimes been viewed as a cocktail because of its diverse origins. Environmentalists come from several different political traditions or none, and they draw together ideas taken from belief systems deriving from a variety of philosophical sources. Some of these have echoes of a back-to-nature style of life, more akin to that of primitive peoples. Others reflect the revolt against industrialisation and economic development of the nineteenth century. Elements of pantheism, romanticism, Malthusianism, anarchism and arguably even fascism have all contributed to strands of green thought.

What greens have done is to weave their specific concerns over matters such as animal rights, conservation, population control and pollution into a coherent and identifiable ideology. Often there is a blending of ecological concerns with other more conventional, human-centred agendas such as conservatism, feminism and socialism. Because of these connections some writers claim that ecology is not new, even if there has never been a synthesis of ecological thinking until the recent past.

ECOLOGISM AND CONSERVATISM

Eco-conservatism establishes the linkage between the cause of conservation and the desire of Conservatives to maintain traditional values and institutions. In particular as Paterson (*Conservation and the Conservatives*) has pointed out:

> *green voters and conservative voters share an instinct for preserving what is good and fine around us and traditional around us. The nature conservationist is a natural conservative.*

As a Tory paternalist he is keen to link his brand of conservatism with the environment. He recognises that the party has always depended for much of its political support on those who live in the countryside, and that the notion of custodianship has a central part in the Conservative approach. According to this view men and women today do not have freeholders' rights to the land in which we live, for we are trustees, obliged to pass on what we inherited from the last generation to the next. Hence the sympathies of Conservatives should be tilted firmly in the direction of those who wish to conserve the best of our environment and to improve the worst of it. Conservation and protection of nature is seen as more moral than neglect or disrespect.

In another way too there are links between conservatism and environmentalism. The eighteenth-century thinker, Edmund Burke, was noted for his disapproval of grand designs and blueprints by which society might be restructured and better organised. His desire was to leave things the way they were, for human societies were seen as too complex, unique and intractable to be successfully tampered with. After all, enduring social practices had developed out of the daily experiences of countless individuals in a variety of circumstances, and were the cumulative results of innumerable adjustments to changing circumstances. The theoretician who would change things risked tampering with this delicate social balance, achieved after much fine-tuning over centuries of trial and error. As with complex ecological systems, even small human interventions can have devastating effects. Burke cautioned repeatedly that:

the nature of man is intricate; the objects of society are of the greatest possible complexity.

Such a preference for conservation and preservation of the status quo can be married with one aspect of green thought.

Rural conservation and a yearning for a pre-industrial past may be beliefs held together. However, the Conservative tradition is in some respects difficult to merge with green thinking. Even paternalistic Conservative-thinking conservatism is anthropocentric as it seeks to modify and adjust (rather than fundamentally restructure) what exists. As Garner notes, dark-green thinking is more 'hands-off' in its approach to nature, less concerned with meeting our needs. It is also guided by an interest in new approaches, and its beliefs are seen as radical in that many greens wish to see a more decentralised form of society in which growth is no longer as important. Limits to growth and small-scale communities do not feature in the Conservative outlook.

The neo-liberal strain of New Right or Thatcherite conservatism might seem to sit uneasily alongside environmental thinking, for it is preoccupied with deregulation, the freedom of market forces and the pursuit of profit which may be harmful to the environment, resulting in pollution and other hazards. Yet there are neo-liberals who argue that it is only through market-based solutions that an answer to environmental hazards can be found. Leach points out that they claim that:

market pressures will oblige entrepreneurs to find innovative alternatives to scarce resources, while experience has demonstrated the profit potential of environmentally-friendly goods. Moreover, ways can be found of making polluters pay.

RADICAL GREEN THINKING

Some environmentalists seek to express their concerns by using the terminology of existing ideologies, so that theories of eco-socialism and eco-feminism exist, as we see on pp 26–28. However, what distinguishes their perspective from that of the socialist or feminist movement is the 'eco', because for ecologists the distinctive feature of their creed is that it rejects the anthropocentric approach of other ideologies. Eco-radical philosophies seek to create new sets of key values and principles which challenge existing assumptions. Whatever the individual strands of environmental thinking, they share a number of eco-radical concerns.

Yet radical environmentalists differ among themselves, with some influenced by a quest for the spiritual values they do not find elsewhere in modern life. Reflective in attitude and gentle in disposition, they sometimes come close to animism, the belief that even inanimate objects are spiritually alive. Some adopt outright paganism. In their view the earth possesses an inherent life-force which, like a living organism, corrects its own imbalances and preserves its global welfare.

Not all ecologists are so gentle, spiritual and even reclusive; some are uncompromising in their ideas and combative in their tactics. They stress that humans are coequal with other species, and our right to live is not inherently distinctive from that of a river to flow as it will, or plants and trees to survive and die. Those who fail to appreciate the rights of other life-forms have set themselves on a collision course with nature, and nature's retaliation for this interference may be ozone depletion and global warming.

Among radical environmentalists or ecologists there are inevitably many shades of opinion. Some of the most important groups are the:

- Social ecologists who argue that hierarchy in society is the key problem; they have links with the anarchist tradition and therefore doubt the abilities of governments to resolve environmental issues.
- Eco-socialists who attack capitalist principles and blame them for causing environmental problems.
- Eco-feminists who blame men for social and environmental destruction.

Social ecologism
Social ecologism is a set of beliefs held by a relatively small if influential group of environmentalists. They are spiritual heirs to the anarchist tradition in politics and take as their starting-point the proven incapacity of the state to come up with

solutions to environmental problems. They argue that all forms of domination are wrong, whether it be of non-human by human or human by human.

Murray Bookchin, an American eco-anarchist, is an exponent of this creed, and he sees social hierarchy in societies as the key problem whether it is based on class, gender or race. Hierarchy is a human construction, and once it is removed, all other forms of domination such as other parts of nature by humans will also disappear. Bookchin allows humans a more exalted place in nature than is common among ecologists, but he opposes any type of domination. Despising the role of the state, he and other social ecologists would abolish it. They favour maximum individual autonomy and decentralised local communities. Dobson observes that this anarchist approach offers 'the closest approximation ... to the centre of gravity of a green sustainable society'.

Eco-socialism

Of course there are many forms of socialism and communism, the creed pre-dating its reformulation by Marx and Friedrich Engels who imparted the economic dimension and class-based view of history. For Marx, socialism focused on social inequality and the consequences of a class-divided capitalist society. It advanced a savage critique of capitalism whose development had produced 'wealth at one pole, misery at the other' and had resulted in an increasingly polarised society.

In Marx's view poverty resulted from capitalism rather than from poor people producing too many offspring. He rejected Malthusian claims that population growth would outstrip the supply of resources, and was hopeful that the better development of productive forces would provide what was necessary. Environmentalists disagree with this unwillingness to accept natural limits.

Yet in some Marxist thought – particularly the earlier works – there are references with which environmentalists would agree. Marx distinguished between progress and capitalist progress; the latter, with its emphasis on making a fast buck, sacrificed the long-term future of natural resources for short-term gain. In his view capitalism was poor stewardship. As he put it:

All progress in capitalistic agriculture is a progress in the art not only of robbing the labourer, but of robbing the soil; all progress towards ruining the lasting sources of that fertility.

Engels too allied his belief in human progress with some understanding of the ecological consequences of that progress:

Let us not flatter ourselves on account of our human victories over nature. For each such victory takes revenge on us. Each victory, it is true, in the first place brings about the results we expected; but in the second and third places, it has quite different and unforeseen effects which only too often cancel the first.

Thus in the outlook of both men there was some wish to combine economic progress with a respect for the natural world.

Today there are many on the Left who remain wary of environmentalism, seeing it as an issue of concern to the privileged middle classes who wish to defend their amenities and rural preservation interests. In this view it has little to do with the lives of urban workers – hence Crosland's remark (see p 4) that there was something elitist in the environmental movement.

Eco-socialists tend to answer such fears by defining the environment widely so that it caters for the concerns of most people. Pepper writes that:

> *[Most] are urban-based so their environmental problems include street violence, vehicle pollution and accidents, inner-city decay, lack of social services, loss of community and access to countryside, health and safety at work, and most important, unemployment and poverty.*

He and others portray eco-socialism as anthropocentric (seeing social injustice as a priority over ecology) and humanist, rejecting the mystification of nature as advanced by many greens. They still see environmental degradation in terms of the failings of capitalism, notably the way in which profit is elevated as the highest good at the expense of all else. They favour state control, the common ownership of the means of production, 'for production is at the centre of our relationship with nature even if it is not the whole of that relationship'.

A number of other socialists feel that socialism and environmentalism can be married, and make the point that there is a common enemy in capitalism. As Weston has put it:

> *It is time that greens accepted that it is capitalism rather than industrialism per se which is at the heart of the problems they address.*

He resents the stress by Porritt and others on the similarities between capitalism and socialism. Bahro also stresses that it is capitalist industrialism which has been the problem because capitalism uses industry to produce for profit rather than need. They suggest that a truly socialist society would produce for need and not for profit, and that consideration of the environment would be integral to policy formation.

Many greens remain unconvinced about the possibility of reconciling Marxism and ecologism, for in Eckersley's phrase it is 'ultimately wedded to the same expansionary ethos and anthropocentric framework as liberalism'. In their view Marx ultimately regarded the non-human world as being the preserve of humans who could use it for their own benefit and seek to impose their own order upon it. Eckersley questions whether Marx ever regarded environmentalism as anything but a peripheral issue.

Of course in one respect it was unfortunate for socialists that the green upsurge of the late 1980s occurred at a time when socialism world-wide was going out of fashion. In its existing form whether in China or Eastern Europe, socialism was under pressure, and the breakdown of the Soviet Union and its satellites enabled writers to pinpoint the failings of socialist societies where environmental damage was often particularly severe. There is no evidence that state control as practised by East European governments was benign in its effect upon the environment.

Eco-feminism

Eco-feminism emerged as a distinct strand of thinking in the 1970s at the time of the rise of the women's liberation movement. In the words of Calassare, eco-feminism refers 'to a feminism that connects ecological degradation and the oppression of women'. Eco-feminists blame much ecological damage on men, male power being the problem. Men are seen as less aware of natural processes and the natural world than women, and eco-feminists believe that there are common strands in the domination of nature and the domination of women.

There are similarities between the women's movement and the environmental one, both being vibrant movements for social change. However, there are many different camps within eco-feminism, the essentialists arguing that women are closer to nature and that this fact should be recognised and developed, whereas constructionists claim that social factors rather than any innate characteristics have done more to shape gender-based inequalities. Essentialists are often seen as more radical eco-feminists, and constructionists more mainstream. The latter find it offensive to suggest that female thought is in any way fundamentally different from male thought, and dislike the idea that women can be identified with nature whilst men are able, in Doyle and McEachern's phrase, 'to appropriate the realms of science and rationality for themselves'.

Much eco-feminist emphasis is on what Garner calls the 'greater affinity [of women] to environmental protection'. Women are seen as closer than men to nature and are therefore more likely to be interested in developing sustainable ways of relating to the environment. He suggests two explanations for this alleged affinity with non-human development:

1 'Women's nurturing role, deriving from their reproductive function, provides for a set of values (of caring and compassion) more conducive to identification with the natural world.'
2 'Women can identify with the environment since they have a mind-set adjusted to oppression...there is an identity of interests between the ending of male exploitation and the ending of human exploitation of the natural environment.'

Radical greens and other creeds

Many deep greens would suggest that although there may be creeds which parade their environmental concerns, much of their approach is at best cosmetic.

For a Conservative or a Socialist the prime concern is the core set of beliefs underpinning their philosophy, and the environment tends to be a peripheral attraction. For the ecologist these concerns are fundamental. The term Earth First!, as taken over by the radical eco-terrorist group (see p 41), sums up the eco-centric viewpoint which stresses that humans must accept that they have no claim to primacy over other species. People need to learn to live in harmony with nature, many of them previously having done things which have posed a direct threat to the long-term survival of the planet.

DOUBTS

In recent years the green message has to some extent been taken on board by many people. However, there is a major difference between the light-green philosophy and lifestyle which many people recognise as desirable, even necessary, for the survival of the planet, and the alternative posed by the various shades of eco-radicals. Few would fully accept the implications of their deep-green approach, and others see the environmentalist case as fundamentally flawed.

Sceptics tend to react against the ideas of purveyors of doom, noting that there have been preachers of fire and brimstone who proclaimed dire warnings of our fate throughout history. In the light of this unreality we should be cautious, not least because:

1 Some green thinkers exaggerate their viewpoint with the intention of alarming people in order to encourage them to accept programmes involving radical solutions.
2 It is easy to forget the capacity of human beings to respond to problems. Human ingenuity and technological advance might provide their own solutions to environmental damage and resource depletion.

Most adherents of other philosophies are committed to economic growth and what they see as the advantages it can offer. They recognise that after so many generations of effort people will not easily give up the good life of material plenty. Writers such as Khan in the USA have reflected this desire for affluence and comfort in modern society, but he has also gone further and poured scorn on the findings and claims of groups such as the Club of Rome; he has projected an alternative and markedly more optimistic scenario for the future of the human race. They deride the suggestion that serious scarcities exist, just as they doubt that there is a serious threat of species extinction. As for the greenhouse effect, the case is unproven and needs more research. In their view those who advance the ecologist case are misguided in their anxieties and unduly alarmist. It is perfectly possible to achieve a balance of environmental concern and the pursuit of desirable economic growth.

Among those who have sought to refute the claims of the environmentalists is a one-time editor of the British science journal *Nature*, John Maddox. Maddox claimed that environmentalists exaggerated the plight of the world by producing a battery of seemingly alarming statistics. He was sceptical about many of the claims made about resource depletion, and economic and population growth, and expressed his faith in science to solve the world's problems. The comparison was drawn between the views of the pessimists and the thinking of Thomas Malthus some two centuries ago. Malthus predicted that the world's population would eventually outstrip its capacity to produce enough food to sustain its growing numbers. He did not forsee that agricultural output would also grow at an increasing rate due to technological innovations.

Similarly to Maddox, Beckerman has suggested that there is no need for anxiety about population levels and other problems. They both believe that human ingenuity and biotechnology can provide the food and other resources the world needs. Along with other writers, Beckerman sees economic growth as the answer to economic and environmental problems, and in the 1980s such free-market solutions were much in vogue in Britain and the USA. Beckerman and other supporters of this school did not deny the importance of environmental matters, but argued that the market could deal with pollution and other problems. They abhorred the notion of governmental action to manage the economy, and saw the dangers of such interventionism as being at least as alarming as the hazards themselves. In their eyes different solutions were possible and inherently superior to any form of state regulation.

Much of the criticism has been anthropocentric. In the view of many sceptics, human beings are not just another species. They may not be the rulers of creation but they have a capacity for rational thought, and can use their intellectual gifts and their understanding of how societies develop to work out desirable forms of progress. If – given this superior rationality and knowledge – he or she decides to re-route a river for agricultural or energy-producing purposes, then what is wrong with that?

It is quite possible for a hierarchical and inegalitarian social system to live in an ecologically sound fashion, so that there is no reason why the only self-sustaining social organisation should be the anarchic commune favoured by deep greens. Adams (*Political Ideology Today*) has expressed a series of doubts about how these communes would relate to each other and how common services would be provided:

Would it not be cost-effective to centralise a number of common functions like the bureaucracy required to issue the Guaranteed Basic Income or hospital care for a number of communities? How would the use of resources be monitored and controlled? Our experience of human nature tells us that some people will always seek to gain a little more than others and will usually be able to find justifications. The Green vision of the future could be a recipe for constant and bitter hostilities between communes. Doesn't history tell us that the strong are likely to bully the weak in order to gain a disproportionate share of the resources? The Bolshevik Revolution was founded on a vision of freely associating self-governing communities but it turned into a totalitarian nightmare. Are not the same seeds of destruction sown in the Green attitude towards social organisation?

Ecological awareness is primarily a Western phenomenon which more advanced and prosperous countries can afford to embrace. This affluence has been achieved as a result of exploitation of the world's resources and befouling of the environment. As the West has achieved success via this route, can we really expect others living in poverty to forgo the blessings which industrial development might bring to improve their overall quality of life? Do we have any right to deny them the opportunities of Western-style advance? The people of the developing world are unlikely to give up such a vision, having enviously viewed it from afar for so long, and might feel that it is time for them to share in the prosperity and comfort.

Some doubt whether we should be thinking of life as it might be a few generations further on. We cannot know what developments will occur in the meantime, and so need to concentrate on the here-and-now. It is unrealistic to expect the current generation to make painful sacrifices for the benefit of future generations whose inhabitants we shall never know. Can we expect people to reduce or even give up their use of the automobile because of its possibly destructive consequences on lifestyles 100 years from now? Other solutions may be found by then. Perhaps the world still lacks the necessary sense of urgency, of imminent catastrophe, to embark on such a fundamental rethinking of our whole way of life.

The vision of committed greens is an essentially utopian one, and in the short term they have to address the issues of everyday life as they seek their ultimately better society. In the meantime they warn of the hazards ahead. The danger they portray is that people will be fully alerted to the prospect of an environmental nightmare when it is too late to do anything about it.

THE DISTINCTIVENESS OF THE GREEN CHALLENGE

Environmentalists differ in their political approach, the differences ranging over beliefs and tactics. Yet all of them have in common a vision of humanity living in accord with the natural world. They believe that we in the Western world are on the wrong track, addicted to our material desires, our consumerist values and our own convenience. We plunder the earth's resources and indulge ourselves in an unnatural lifestyle in which we eat processed food, travel by means which pollute the atmosphere, and are preoccupied with the gadgetry of modern living, from fluorescent lights to television, freezers to air conditioning. They posit an alternative lifestyle in which people live in harmony with the natural world and respond to the sun, wind, air and earth, and in which we return to the elemental pleasures which are available for the use of humanity and all other living species.

Whereas moderate environmentalists are interested in the protection and preservation of nature for the benefit of society, it is the eco-centrism of the radical environmentalist critique which makes it especially distinctive. Ecologism is based on certain assumptions about the relationship of humankind and nature, and fundamental to these is the belief that the natural world is not a convenient resource provided for us to exploit. It offers an eco-centric future in which the human species is part of – rather than master of – nature.

SUMMARY

- *Conservation* involves the protection, preservation and careful management of the world's resources. It refers primarily to natural resources, but within the conservation movement we would include organisations such as the National Trust which wishes to preserve fine buildings as well as areas of outstanding natural beauty.
- *Environmentalism* is also concerned with protection. Environmentalists are alarmed by the damage and destruction caused by the nature and pace of economic development. However, moderates among them approach ecological problems in a measured and pragmatic way. They accept much of the ecologists' diagnosis and are appropriately humble in the face of nature. But, they do not believe that all species have the same rights, and can accept human beings as having superior wisdom and privileges; they tend to be anthropocentric. They see ecological issues as involving delicate balances and difficult choices between human welfare and environmental obligations. They do not embrace the anti-technological stance of their more radical associates.
- *Ecologism* is concerned with the relationship of living organisms and their environment, and its adherents speak of the interconnectedness of nature and the network of relationships which sustain all forms of life. Ecologists (or radical environmentalists) are eco-centric; they see human beings as part of nature, not its masters in the way that the *Book of Genesis* proclaims.

STUDY GUIDES

Revision Hints

In your notes you need to define what ideology is, and know the meaning of terms such as conservation, environmentalism and ecologism. Then, set out in list form the main tenets of the moderate and radical environmentalists, and add a paragraph or two on the ways in which ecology (radical environmentalism) can overlap with other creeds. You should be in a position to work out why some Conservatives, Socialists, feminists and anarchists in particular can identify with green attitudes. At the end write down a summary of any ideas which seem specifically green ones, ie thoughts which make it possible to claim that ecology is a distinctive ideology.

Exam Hints

Questions on green thinking are becoming more common on papers dealing with political ideas. The topic is usually included within a section of textbooks which deals with contemporary ideological currents, often as part of a section on new radical creeds such as feminism and various types of liberation ideology.

There are, then, two broad types of question which focus on the more recent kinds of radical thinking. Various green writers have taken up ecology after a flirtation with various New Left creeds in the 1960s, and they have seen their ecological concerns as an extension of their New Left ideas; in their view green thinking marks the culmination of the radicalism of the 1960s. Hence a question such as the one below enables you to include green thought along with material relating to liberation of oppressed groups dealing with issues surrounding women and animals:

'As with the ideas underlying the animal-rights movement and feminism, the concerns that lie behind green thinking are not entirely new.' To what extent do these ideological positions develop, and to what extent do they depart from, the main traditions of earlier social and political creeds?

More orthodox questions are concerned with the distinctiveness of green thinking. They require you to understand the extent to which environmentalists of all shades draw upon other doctrines. In other words, is green thinking an amalgam of elements of various ancient and more recent eighteenth- and nineteenth-century ideas, or does it have something unique to offer?

Members of the group can each take up one element of thinking under the environmentalist umbrella, ranging from the attitudes of light greens and dark greens to those of eco-socialists and eco-feminists. Each can offer an explanation as to why Conservatives or Socialists can in some cases identify with green thinking, and point out the problems involved in effecting any such reconciliation.

A debate could be organised on the motion that:

This house believes that the adoption of shallow environmentalism will not be sufficient to save the planet.

1   Is environmentalism a single, distinctive doctrine?
2   In what respects do environmentalists depart from conventional political thinking?

Animal liberation   A philosophical (ideological) position which argues against speciesism, the doctrine that only human beings possess rights (see below).

Animism   The belief that natural objects, phenomena and the universe itself possess souls.

Anthropocentric   Regarding human beings as the most important and central part of the universe, and therefore according their priority over other species.

Bio-centric/Eco-centric   A doctrine which prioritises the maintenance and ecological balance rather than the satisfaction of human interests. The opposite of anthropocentrism, it stresses the interconnectedness of all forms of life, humans being a part of nature not its masters.

Biosphere   The part of the earth's surface and atmosphere inhabited by living things.

Cornucopia   A place of abundance.

Eco-radical philosophies   Philosophies which aim to create new sets of values which challenge existing assumptions, eg about our role in nature.

Eco-terrorist   An extremist within the environmental movement who is prepared to carry out terrorist acts against companies, industries and other workplaces if he or she feels that unnecessary damage to the environment is being caused.

Ecology   The study of the relationships between living organisms and their environment. As a political doctrine, it supports the bio-centric view that there is an essential link between human beings and the natural world which are both part of the oneness of nature.

Environmentalist   Someone committed to maintaining the ecological balance and the conservation of the environment. Moderate environmentalists ultimately see nature as serving our interests whereas radical environmentalists (ecologists) wish to protect nature for non-human reasons and take a bio-centric perspective.

Gaia   The goddess of the earth, who bore Uranus, and by him Oceanus, Cronus and the Titans. A strand of green thinking accords Gaia a supreme place, Gaia being – in the words of Lovelock – 'Earth's biosphere, atmosphere, oceans and soil'. Gaia is a living organism which acts to maintain its own existence.

Greens   Supporters of green politics covering a variety of environmental and ecological causes, who employ a variety of political strategies, from the parliamentary to the violent, to achieve their end of preserving the natural environment.

Malthusian claims   The claims of Malthus 200 years ago that the increase in population would outstrip the supply of food and resources to sustain it.

Speciesism   The anthropocentric view that nature is to be aggressively mastered by humans.

Further Reading

Adams, I. (1993) *Political Ideology Today*, MUP
Ashby, E. (1978) *Reconciling Man with the Environment*, OUP
Dobson, A. (1990) *Green Political Thought: An Introduction*, Allen and Unwin
Doyle, T. and McEachern, D. (1998) *Environment and Politics*, Routledge
Eckersley, R. (1992) *Environmentalism and Political Theory*, UCL
Garner, R. (1996) *Environmental Politics*, Harvester Wheatsheaf
Heywood, A. (1998) *Political Ideologies: An Introduction*, Macmillan
Leach, R. (1996) *British Political Ideologies*, Harvester Wheatsheaf
Meadows, D., Randers, D. and Behrens, W. (1972) *The Limits to Growth*, Earthscan
Robinson, M. (1992) *The Greening of British Politics*, MUP

3

GREEN MOVEMENTS AND PRESSURE GROUPS

Introduction

WITHIN OUR DEMOCRATIC system there are a wide variety of organised interests and causes represented by pressure groups. The interplay of these interests is an important feature of present-day government.

Environmental groups and movements have experienced an impressive rate of growth over the last generation. They have made effective use of the media to advance discussion of green issues, and via the European Union have acquired a new channel through which to seek political influence. Such organisations are very important in environmental politics, for because of the failure of the Green Party to make significant headway, pressure-group activity and direct action seem to provide a more productive area of activity.

Key Points
As you read this chapter, ask yourself:

- How would you distinguish between a movement and a pressure group?
- Why are environmental movements often referred to as new social movements?
- What do you think is the most convincing way of classifying environmentalist pressure groups?
- Why do some environmental activists favour lobbying the EU or the use of direct action as a means of pressing their claims?
- Why have rural issues been such a feature of environmental activity in recent years?

MOVEMENTS AND THEIR CHARACTERISTICS

Movements are different from interest or pressure groups but often closely related to them; difficulties can arise in discovering the exact nature of the relationship. As Grant explains:

> *When pressure group activity springs from a social movement, it may thus reflect the characteristics of that movement although, clearly, individuals subscribing to a broad goal – such as the abolition of hunting – may differ about how that goal should be achieved.*

A movement may be described as a large body of people united, but loosely organised, around a central idea, issue or concern whose goal is to change attitudes or institutions, as well as policies. Their activities often arise at grass-roots level and later evolve into national crusades. Within our definition, we may speak of the civil rights movement in the USA, the women's movement and the anti-abortion movement. These groups operate in a political terrain which is quite distinct from more established and institutionalised political forms such as parties and pressure groups, and it was within these non-institutional, more informal realms of society and its politics that environmental movements emerged.

New movements arise from time to time as people discover new needs and the old ones become satisfied. For instance, in the 1990s one of the more vocal and militant is the animal rights movement which, as Garner points out, has adopted:

> *a wide range of direct action strategies … This has most notably included breaking into factory farms and laboratories where the animals may be released, equipment destroyed and evidence of ill-treatment compiled … The Animal Liberation Front … consists of autonomous cells of activists and, for obvious reasons, has no hierarchical organisation structure.*

NEW SOCIAL MOVEMENTS

Environmentalism was born in environmental movements. Doyle and McEachern describe their characteristics clearly:

> *[Such] groups … inject themselves into politics and challenge dominant ideas and a given constellation of power … In contemporary parlance, [the] labour movement of the nineteenth century (people who united to confront harsh working conditions and pressed for change) would be seen as an example of an old social movement in contrast to the 'new' social movements, which include both the women's movement and the environmental movement. These are new in the*

> *sense that they challenge a new set of dominant ideas and another constellation of power ... Like the preceding social movements they have a radical edge and visions of a world transformed by their demands ... [They] are characterised by their informal modes of organisation; their attachment to changing values as a central part of their political challenge; their commitment to open and ultra-democratic, participating modes of organisation (at least in the initial stages) and their willingness to engage in direct action to stop outcomes which they see as harmful.*

Different environmentalists have different goals, their conclusions reflecting their ideological beliefs, personal interests and the areas in which they operate. Within the broad umbrella there are several movements that share some but not all of their concerns. Those who see themselves as part of the movement sometimes disagree on certain tactics, even though they may agree on the broad goals to be pursued.

Sometimes movements may feel left out of government and may resort to extreme measures to advance their cause. Often their members do not acknowledge the routines of conventional party politics, seeing political parties as largely irrelevant in their bid to push their particular concerns to the forefront of political debate. They believe that they have superior values and want to see a shift of priorities in society so that we move away from the present materialistic preoccupations into a post-materialist age. Arguments related to the aesthetic values of nature, the rights of non-humans, and ecology are part of this approach. But of course in poorer parts of the world, environmental movements may have other priorities more related to survival and security in conditions worsened by environmental misuse and damage. The struggles of the Ogoni peoples of Nigeria against the environmental degradation brought about by the activities of Shell Oil are an example of this different type of environmental movement.

Around the world, environmental movements differ considerably in their general and specific goals as well as in their internal organisation. They are complex to analyse, being often rather amorphous in their structures and constantly being refashioned as new issues appear on the agenda and others fade away.

In the eyes of the outside world, there is one broad environmental movement in each region, country or continent, but those in the know would distinguish several different ones. Doyle and McEachern refer to two types:

1 **Traditional nature–conservation movements.** The main thrust of the nature-conservation movement is to protect species in danger of extinction in a modernising world. They are often in the forefront of the fight against pollution. They are content to operate within the existing economic order by proposing moderate reforms and ensuring that politics has a 'green tinge'.
2 **New-Left movements.** In contrast the New-Left movements seek dramatic change in which ecological and social needs are seen as more important than

economic concerns of the existing pattern of society, in particular the obsession with economic growth. The anti-nuclear movement is an offshoot of the political ecology campaign, often sharing similar membership and a common outlook. Its main preoccupation is with the danger posed by nuclear power stations and the search for alternative energy sources. Within its orbit the emphasis has been on decentralisation and individual or small group activity, sometimes of a more radical and unconventional kind.

BRITAIN AND THE REST OF WESTERN EUROPE

Many of the most well-known environmental movements are based in Western Europe. In Britain from the 1970s onwards, members of environmental movements began to operate through an array of often local and national networks, individuals and organisations to advance their beliefs. Their activities varied in kind from blockades and marches to more tranquil activities such as lobbying for policy changes and new initiatives.

The fragmentation of particular environmental movements into such groups and networks reflects the range of differing approaches to matters of ideology and policy, as well as differing views on the best means to employ to achieve them. Membership is fluid because movements include many individuals who are not necessarily members of individual organisations such as pressure groups, yet who provide broad support. Hence the constant state of flux in which movements exist. Whatever their fortunes, without the environmental movements and their offshoots there would be little or no greening of government and corporations.

THE UNITED STATES

In the USA environmental movements have been less rooted in ecology and nuclear issues, and more concerned with nature conservation. In this respect they are more akin to Doyle's first category although the emphasis is on what he calls 'wilderness-oriented perspectives'. They are less preoccupied with the environment as it has evolved and more concerned with issues regarding the fate of wolves and grizzly bears, the management of national parks and the protection of species of fauna. This wilderness-orientation exists particularly in the western regions where there are still large tracts of land which are relatively undeveloped. In the east, matters of air and water quality rate more highly.

There are more radical groups which voice more challenging theses and emphasise the importance of direct action, but their activities are untypical of US movements as a whole.

PRESSURE-GROUP ACTIVITY

Having examined environmental movements, we move on to a study of environmental pressure groups, which are more visible players on the environmental scene. Matters of definition are again important, and some writers use the term NGOs (non-governmental organisations) to describe the huge range of bodies which exist and operate on the local, national and international scene. The term NGO can be used to include business interests represented by the commercial private sector, for some firms are keen to advance their green credentials as they make policy. Such claims are viewed with scepticism by others in the green movement, and the efforts of business persons are generally viewed as self-interested and beyond the realms of genuine environmental concern; indeed often they are seen as a hindrance to the advancement of green ideas.

In recent decades there has developed a plethora of NGOs in the environmental field, ranging from myriads of small bodies to much more well-known organisations. They are political organisations and usually have constitutions which set out their intentions, mode of internal organisation and external operation. They are playing the political game and therefore they are usually in the business of working within the dominant structures of the state. Radical activists who are to be found in the broader environmental movements are often less interested in participating in this type of activity, for the world of lobbying and mainstream politics is not to their liking. They tend to be wary of politicians whose motives they suspect, and themselves prefer to operate in less conventional ways.

Writers on British politics usually refer to pressure groups rather than NGOs, and this is the term we will generally employ here as we distinguish distinctive types of organisation. Some pressure groups are global players such as Greenpeace, based in Amsterdam, and FoE which originated in the USA. Many are national organisations, ranging from the Sierra Club in the USA to the Campaign for Lead Free Air (CLEAR) and the National Trust in Britain.

Estimates of the number of environmental pressure groups across the world vary considerably, partly depending on the definition adopted. Porter and Brown detected 13,000 in the developed world and 2,230 in the developing countries in their study based on work done in the early 1980s. The number accelerated later in that decade, and by 1990 there were some 530 in 45 countries in the African NGOs Environment Network (ANEN) alone. Doyle and McEachern quote figures of 12,000 NGOs in India, 10,000 in Bangladesh and 6,000 in Latin America. Not only was there a mushrooming in the number of associations, there was also a surge in the membership of many of them. Of the more prominent, Greenpeace, FoE and the Sierra club experienced huge growth.

This explosion of environmental pressure group activity world-wide lost some of its impetus in the 1990s, particularly in Britain and some other countries affected by economic recession. After a period of expansion, there may have been an inevitable levelling off of activity as groups consolidated their gains and concentrated more on adopting policy positions and the pursuit of their goals than on membership drives.

THE VARIETY OF GROUPS INVOLVED

Many factors contribute to the variety of pressure-group activity in the environmental field. These include: their location, ideology, size, target of influence, method of campaigning and funding. Whereas an organisation such as Greenpeace favours mass mobilisation, has some 5 million members world-wide and has funded itself via membership drives and sometimes controversial direct marketing techniques, Earth First! – an organisation which shares a radical deep-green ideology and a willingness to use direct action – has a smaller membership which is difficult to quantify, operates mainly at a regional or local level and shows a greater willingness to engage in more violent means of direct action.

Many groups are much less well known, and among the myriad of them there are those:

- Which favour resource conservation, eco-feminism and deep ecology.
- Which operate at a global level or in the national political arena, and those which are primarily involved in some community controversy.
- With vast memberships such as the 100,000 of the Australian group Australian Conservation Foundation (ACF), and tiny bodies such as the 40 who belong to Zedon (Green Don), a Russian group based in the vicinity of the Black Sea.

ENVIRONMENTAL PRESSURE GROUPS IN BRITAIN

In Britain the term 'pressure groups' is frequently used to cover the range of organisations of which we speak, although other terms such as interest groups and the lobby are often employed as well. Pressure groups are associations other than political parties which attempt directly or indirectly to influence the decisions of government.

Distinctions between parties and pressure groups cannot be absolutely foolproof, but broadly, parties exist with the intention of pursuing political power so that they can run the government. Pressure groups do not wish to run the government, though they may seek to influence it by putting pressure on public officials or members of the legislature. Whereas parties tend to have broad, moderate programmes designed to appeal to a majority of the electorate, pressure groups have narrower ones, of interest to a specialised clientele. Their membership is often limited to one section of the community.

The connection between parties and pressure groups may be a close one, and sometimes the differences between them are blurred. Some environmental groups such as FoE have put up candidates in by-elections, more to achieve publicity than in the expectation of victory. In general, however, the distinction is clear. Although farmers have sometimes discussed the possibility of organising a separate party, the National Farmers' Union (NFU) has generally regarded the idea as impracticable and over-ambitious. Agrarian parties have at times flourished in countries which have used proportional representation to elect members of their legislatures (such as Scandinavia), but today they are uncommon. British agriculturists have taken the pressure group route to advance their interests.

AN ATTEMPT AT CLASSIFICATION

There is a multiplicity of pressure groups, and several attempts have been made at classification. Finer distinguished between groups involved in different areas of activity, such as 'civic' groups, and 'educational, recreational and cultural' ones. More usually, writers choose the distinction made by Stewart in *British Pressure Groups* and subsequently modified by others. Different names are sometimes invoked, but the broad lines of delineation are clear enough, between those which protect their members and those which seek to promote a cause not of immediate benefit to themselves.

Protective groups

These are usually permanent, with a mass membership, and they provide services for their members as well as demanding sacrifices from them; they defend a section of society. In the environmental field, examples are difficult to find if only because people who support the environment tend to be altruistic in their concerns rather than self-interested. However, the NFU and the Country Landowners' Association have an obvious interest in the protection of the countryside, although their perspective is very different from that of the many green activists who abhor some of their farming techniques. Because of the nature of their task and those whom they represent, both groups are described as interest, defensive or sectional groups. So too are the British Veterinary Association and the Royal College of Veterinary Surgeons.

Promotional groups

Unlike the protective organisations, the members of promotional groups do not stand to gain directly from what they seek to achieve. They want to advance a cause by appealing not to a section of the community but to everybody, in the hope of promoting a policy of general benefit rather than of personal advantage. Thus the CPRE wants to see rural England better preserved, the League Against Cruel Sports is concerned about the mistreatment of animals, and the Conservation Society campaigns for the preservation of fine buildings and other features of our national heritage. Such groups, sometimes known as propaganda, ideas or cause groups, tend to be less powerful than interest ones; they have limited funds and few if any permanent staff. In some cases they have a tendency to split into rival factions.

Hybrid groups

There are also some **hybrid groups** which may be established by interest groups but exist to promote a cause. The Noise Abatement Society has members whose primary concern is to safeguard the environment; yet it also contains manufacturers of equipment to suppress noise – they have an economic interest in noise abatement.

More recently, Grant has produced a typology of groups based on their relationship to central decision-makers. He is concerned with whether a particular group has access to the corridors of power, and thus divides groups according to whether they are insider or outsider ones:

- **Insider groups** are regarded as legitimate by government and are consulted on a regular basis.
- **Outsider groups** either do not wish to become enmeshed in a consultative relationship with officials, or are unable to gain recognition.

Another way of looking at outsider groups is to see them as protest groups which have objectives that are outside the mainstream of political opinion. They need to adopt campaigning methods designed to demonstrate that they have a solid basis of popular support.

Many protective groups such as the NFU are insiders, and some, including the NFU, have consultative status. Similarly, promotional groups are often outsider ones, but there are several exceptions such as the CPRE and the Royal Society for the Protection of Birds (RSPB) which are in frequent touch with representatives of government. The World Wide Fund for Nature is, in Garner's view:

> *the classic example of an insider group which uses its conservation expertise as a means of gaining access to governments throughout the world.*

If groups move towards more institutionalised and moderate stances in this way, as has happened with FoE and even to some extent with Greenpeace, they do of course run the risk of being outflanked by new, more radical groups such as Earth First! whose members are prepared to take direct action.

Not all writers favour the Grant typology, for as Whiteley and Winyard (*Pressure for the Poor*) point out:

> *Some groups can enjoy close contacts with Whitehall yet at the same time make considerable use of the media and public strategies of protest; they are insiders in terms of status, but outsiders in terms of strategy.*

Hence Maloney et al (*Journal of Public Administration*, vol. 14:1) distinguish between insider, outsider and thresholder groups; the latter being 'characterised by strategic ambiguity and oscillation between insider and outsider strategies'. Both the National Trust and English Heritage have in recent years been increasingly willing to supplement their behind-the-scenes (insider) tactics with recourse to the media, thus possibly entitling them to thresholder status.

WIND POWER: A CASE STUDY OF GROUP CLASSIFICATION

There are several means by which writers have attempted to categorise environmental groups other than by the more general protective/promotional classification, which can be applied to those operating in any area of activity. For instance, back in 1982 Cotgrove made the distinction between *conservationist* ones such as the National Trust and the RSPB which he viewed as Right-inclined, and the *new environmentalists* such as FoE and Greenpeace who were Left-leaning.

In much literature, discussions about differences between environmentalists have been dominated by a distinction between those who are said to focus primarily on how human interests are affected, and those who take an overview which places the interests of nature as the prime focus of their ecology. As we have seen, the former position is called *anthropocentrism* and the latter *eco-centrism*. A continuum is said to exist between these positions. Broadly, *light green* is equivalent to anthropocentric, and eco-centric is equivalent to *deep green*.

Toke has criticised both of the above approaches. In his research into wind power, he has tried applying the Cotgrove analysis and finds that it is inadequate. Wind power is more likely to be supported by the new environmentalists than by more conservative groups, although the RSPB is not strongly opposed to it whereas many landscape conservationists are. He stresses the importance of the issue itself, and remarks that: 'What is crucial is how the various groups see their interests being affected by the deployment of wind power.'

He is similarly unimpressed by classifications which emphasise differences over ideology. Again they fail to show how groups disagree on specific issues because of the divergent interests which support them. He has found that the deep-green–light-green continuum does not provide a completely satisfactory understanding of the conflict over wind power. True, the main opposition to windfarm proposals has been on the human-centred grounds that they destroy the landscape value, and may also produce high noise levels. But damage to wildlife may be caused when foundations for wind turbines have to be installed, roads have to be laid for access and there is a possible threat to birds from turning blades; these are disadvantages which conservationists would be expected to air. He concludes that green politics are too complex to be represented by a single ideological divide.

Toke favours a classification based on *policy interests*, which enables him to study wind power in terms of the divergence of interests between different environmental groups. He finds that FoE and Greenpeace have promoted wind power along with anti-nuclear groups and organisations; indeed, the policy became 'an icon of the green movement' in the 1970s and 1980s. However, rural groups such as the Council for the Protection of Rural Wales have become increasingly hostile to proposals to wind power schemes, and in many English branches too there is unease about their effects. The Ramblers' Association and the Council for National Parks are also fearful of the greater use of wind power, for they know that the windiest sites often have the greatest landscape value. Their views have been buttressed by a specifically anti-wind-power organisation, the National Campaign Against Windfarms. Local action groups have similarly joined in the attack, often again for landscape reasons.

Toke shuns any attempt to classify pressure groups according to their ideology, political leanings or tactics. Instead, he favours a *localist/sectionalist/globalist* classification.

- **Localist groups** are concerned with issues specific to their localities.
- **Sectionalist groups** may be national or international in character but are mainly concerned with one policy area.
- **Globalist groups** are concerned with a full range of issues.

This model is then applied to the issue of wind power as a tool of analysis to show how the differing interests of environmental groups conflict.

Many localist groups have focused on landscape issues because of the affluent middle-class professionals and retired persons who often inhabit the countryside and do not wish to see their lifestyle threatened. Sectionalist groups include many of those formed in the late nineteenth century which sought to defend specific aspects of natural and historic beauty, such as the National Trust. They have interests concerned with the environment in more than one locality, as do Compassion for World Farming and the anti-road-building group, Alarm UK. Globalist groups, a more recent variety, include FoE and Greenpeace. Their preoccupations may vary, but in common they have both the fact of their broad concern about a number of environmental problems which threaten the planet, and their demand for a radical change in the social systems of many countries.

In the case of wind power, there is an alliance on the 'anti' side between local groups opposed to particular projects, and various sectionalist ones who concentrate on landscape issues. Globalist groups – and some sectionalist ones – support wind power. It all depends on how a group's interests are affected by the issue. Rather than concentrating on ideological divisions as represented by adherents of different strands of green thought, it is better to be practical and analyse the behaviour and motives of the doers.

SOURCE: ADAPTED FROM D. TOKE'S PAPER TO THE CONFERENCE OF THE POLITICAL STUDIES ASSOCIATION, 1998

THE METHODS BY WHICH PRESSURE GROUPS OPERATE

Pressure groups have traditionally operated at three main levels, and the approach adopted depends on the type of group involved. Large, powerful protective groups have close contacts in **Whitehall**, for it is in the government departments that key decisions are made. It is the higher civil service which offers advice to the minister, the political head of a government department, and so it is very worthwhile to contact senior civil servants or if possible see a junior minister or his or her boss. Civil servants/ministers find the lobby (the network of groups with whom they are in dialogue) helpful. They can get technical information and advice, and maybe help in carrying out a policy.

In return the groups learn the department's current thinking and hope to influence its decisions and get bills drawn up following their recommendations. Much of this contact is regular and formalised, but frequent phone calls will be made, eg between the NFU and the Ministry of Agriculture, Fisheries and Food (MAFF). The NFU, which values its consultative status in Whitehall, operates in a way which avoids publicity, and only when a row breaks out will it turn to open public methods.

Interest groups may also have contacts in **Westminster** where many promotional groups possibly have some spasmodic support. If an MP draws a high position in the annual ballot to introduce a private member's bill, many groups will rush to contact him or her in the hope that a measure relating to their cause will be introduced. They may have one ready or else help him or her draft one (eg the anti-blood-sports groups are usually keen to find someone willing to introduce legislation in accordance with their preferences, hence the ill-fated Foster Bill of 1997–98).

Promotional groups also try to persuade popular opinion in their favour in the hope that the press and MPs will then take up their cause if it proves to be one of much concern. Above all, they wish to influence **the public** who are the voters in the next election. The coming of television has provided opportunities for much more publicity, and some groups now campaign in this way, often using **direct action** (see pp 51–53).

Since the 1970s, the key development has been that in addition to pursuing these avenues, pressure groups have increasingly turned their attention to **Europe** (see also Chapter 6). With the passage of the Single European Act and the opening up of the single market, more and more decisions are being taken in Brussels. For several years some of the larger sectional groups have found this a fertile area for their lobbying activity. The European Commission is a relatively open bureaucracy, and the views of various interests are carefully considered in the early stages of draft legislation; MEPs and party groupings are also the focus of some attention, MEPs being a useful avenue through which more attention can be paid to the Commission.

Groups ranging from the NFU to the RSPCA and from FoE to the British Veterinary Association are effective at the European level. Approaches vary according to the resources of the group and type of issue, but three broad methods of pressure can be applied to the EU:

1 *Lobbying the British government* to encourage it to use its influence in the Council of Ministers, an approach much used by the NFU on matters of farm prices and the Common Agricultural Policy (CAP) in general.
2 *Acting through a Euro-group* representing pressure groups across the Union, again an avenue used by the NFU via the Committee of Professional Agricultural Associations. Of the Euro-groups, the Federation of Veterinarians of the European Union has many sub-committees dealing with issues such as animal welfare and mutilation, and food hygiene.
3 *Making direct contact with the European machinery*, particularly the European Parliament and the Commission. Some groups such as the NFU go further; since Britain joined the European Community, it has maintained an office in Brussels.

US ENVIRONMENTAL GROUPS

For several years, US commentators have noted that the environment has become a growth area in pressure group activity. Some older bodies have been reinvigorated and spread their organisation to the states, and new ones have emerged – some of which place more emphasis on the role of direct action.

Many groups work within the mainstream of Washington politics and have well-staffed offices which lobby in the capital. The Group of Ten organisations between them have a vast budget and more than 5 million members. They include the Environmental Defense Fund, FoE, National Wildlife Federation and Sierra Club. The largest is the Wildlife Federation with over 3 million members and funds of nearly $100 million, whereas FoE has a much smaller membership of around 50,000 and a budget of $2–3 million.

The Group of Ten is scorned by some in the green movement, for they portray its leading activists as 'limousine environmentalists' who work too closely with the existing political system rather than acting as radicals seeking to transform society. They distrust the cosy relationship with spokespersons for industry and government. Of the more radical groups which support the use of direct action, Earth First! has already been mentioned. It advocates and executes attacks on equipment used on construction sites, and its members resort to tree-spiking to prevent the logging of trees – even at the risk of causing serious injury to the loggers involved. Supporters of Sea Shepherd interfere with the activities of large fishing and whaling craft.

More traditional associations often made use of the courts in the heydays of the 1960s and early 1970s, and still this can be effective. Public Citizen, the Sierra

Club and FoE recently brought a case in the federal courts to require the North America Free Trade Treaty (NAFTA) to include a clear statement on the importance of environmental protection measures within the agreement, an issue on which Canadian and US groups made common cause (such a transnational alliance in group activity has also been employed in the debate over acid-rain fall-out from power plants, a debate which brought the governments of the two countries into conflict).

Generally speaking, in more recent years US groups have concentrated their attention more on the legislatures at federal and state level. They have lobbied elected representatives to defend protection legislation when it is under assault. They have also paid more attention to the executive branch, seeking to persuade leading staff of the importance of their concerns. Twenty years ago their case was accepted without the same degree of caution as is now applied.

Groups can meet considerable resistance to their ideas. In the North-west woodlands, both labour and management in the lumber industry are hostile to the efforts of those environmentalists who campaign to save the forested areas. Companies argue that if they cannot cut down trees, then they will be driven into bankruptcy. They point to the detrimental results that their failure will have not just for the staff they employ but also for the economy of the region – for instance on costs in the building trade.

CITIZEN POWER IS A POWERFUL FORCE ON BOTH SIDES OF THE ATLANTIC ON ISSUES SUCH AS NUCLEAR POWER

Francis (*Developments in American Politics*) has demonstrated that the environmental lobby is now a powerful force in the US policy process, the more so given the presence of green activists within the Democratic Party. Yet despite the widespread sympathy for the cause:

> *economic concerns set limits to that sympathy. The unresolved issues of environmental protection and economic growth have now become all the more urgent as American politics are increasingly affected by decisions taken beyond the United States border.*

USE OF DIRECT ACTION

In a democracy, if people feel that no-one in authority is listening to their case or that government is unresponsive to their wishes, they may be tempted to adopt more coercive tactics. Groups seeking political change, finding that the normal channels are not achieving the desired outcome, may resort to unconstitutional means – those contrary to the spirit of our unwritten constitution – such as deliberate law-breaking and/or violence. By direct action, strictly speaking, we mean doing for yourself what the government has refused to do. Baggott has described it as a situation when a group:

> *takes matters into its own hands rather than relying on established methods of decision-making, to resolve a problem.*

By extension, the term now refers to any attempt to coerce the government or those in authority into a change of viewpoint.

In recent years a number of environmental groups have seen benefit in using direct action as an additional means of persuading ministers into following their ideas. By so doing they achieve publicity, for the television cameras are likely to be present at some mass protest or demonstration. Of course, noise and publicity are not the same as influence, and it is still true that for some organisations, resorting to such forms of demonstration is an indication of weakness rather than strength. However, many local action and promotional groups have used direct action as an additional tool. There are many examples of the Nimby type of groups (see overleaf) which have used this to block attempts to build a housing estate on green-belt land or to block the felling of some ancient tree in the name of progress.

There is a continuum of forms of pressure which may develop, starting with more peaceful forms of protest, and then escalating to threats, strikes, boycotts, demonstrations, riots and rebellion. Non-violent direct action may include a number of extra-parliamentary methods which are peaceful and designed to achieve changes in the law or in government policies after more usual constitutional procedures have failed to achieve their purpose. Often these are not unconstitutional or illegal in any strict sense, but there is the possibility that the events or approach may get out of hand and spill over into something more threatening. Some direct action shuns the more passive form of protest, legal or illegal, and seeks to attain its end by the use of force, as when animal rights protestors invade a laboratory or some group uses arson or bomb attacks against a member of the government.

Media interest has recently focused on the behaviour and lifestyle of individuals such as Daniel Hooper (Swampy) and the causes they espouse. They have operated in areas such as anti-bypass and anti-airport campaigning. In the words of one writer in *The Guardian*, they have become cool. However, their sometimes-small group activities are but one aspect of the environmental protest scene, and a wide range of groups have resorted to direct action, including organisations such as Critical Mass and Greenpeace. Whether it be the use of street parties on barricaded roads to highlight the problems of traffic and road safety, the protests against live animal exports at Brightlingsea or the actions at Newbury and Twyford Down, the intention is the same. It is to bring issues to public attention which ministers and others in authority would prefer to keep quiet and ignore. The use of direct action may disrupt and hinder plans, make progress on schemes costly and unpopular, and help to force those in authority to rethink their ideas.

NIMBY GROUPS

Nimby groups are difficult to classify, for they are primarily self-interested in that they wish to protect their local areas from the encroachments of predatory developers, yet they have an open membership. They are often joined in their campaigns by many other activists who are more interested in making a general stand against an excess of motorway building, the destruction of communities and the felling of trees, than in emphasising purely immediate matters.

The groups usually operate at local level, although sometimes they have been established in response to decisions taken by national governments or multinational companies. Much of their work is concerned with amending, delaying or blocking new developments, particularly affecting housing and the siting of industry and transport (rail-road links, the Channel Tunnel etc). Baggott quotes the example of Mothers and Children Against Toxic Waste (MACATV), a Welsh group which campaigned to prevent a local chemical plant from burning toxic waste. Nuclear waste is a well-known arena for Nimby activity, as local residents fight to fend off the nearby location of a site for dealing with radioactive material; thus Lincolnshire Against Nuclear Dumping (LAND) opposed governmental plans for the disposal of low-level nuclear substances.

Nimby groups are self-interested in that they are concerned to defend the lifestyles of local residents. But this is a legitimate reason for taking action. Even if a project is desirable on wider economic and social grounds, it may be unfair if a number of people bear the main brunt of any disadvantage incurred; at the very least they may deserve generous compensation. Moreover they help to draw public attention to more general threats posed to the environment, and in as much as they do draw in outsiders, they can help gain wide publicity about the problems caused by road-building programmes and the priorities attached to such policies as supermarket development.

Many of the environmentalist protesters have been willing to be obstructive, and the more zealous among them have resorted to violence, which they regard as a necessary and effective way of combating official obstinacy and structural force. In their view, the time for bargaining is over, given the magnitude of the issues and the implications of the decisions which they are confronting and challenging. Hoad (*Talking Politics*, vol. 10:3) points out that in their eyes the issues of 'destruction of natural habitat and species depletion' and many others are so serious in their implications that 'only by taking a pro-active stance will anything be accomplished'.

For moderate environmentalists, the regular, even persistent, use of illegal and violent direct action gives the cause a bad name. They are prepared to boycott goods, block roads and impede the movement of goods at dockyards, even to the point of inviting arrest, but such methods as syringing cans of food, releasing mink or digging up the graves of former hunt leaders are seen as beyond the pale. What is significant, however, is the way in which the environmental movement has managed on several occasions to unite both moderates and radicals in the same campaign. Baggott quotes *The Campaigning Handbook*:

The Twyford Down protest for example was strengthened by informal alliances with local conservatives, and the radical-traditional axis has become a feature of protests since.

Certainly, in anti-motorway protests, in the struggles to halt the export of live animals and abolish hunting, and in the unsuccessful bid to fend off the possibility of a second runway at Manchester Airport, the regular activists who move from site to site and the respectable middle classes, worried by a threat to their traditional amenities and lifestyle, have made common cause.

IS DIRECT ACTION JUSTIFIABLE IN A DEMOCRACY?

In a perfect democracy, everyone would be equally free to secure consideration of his or her interests and would accept the fairness of the result. But many individuals and groups feel that the traditional political processes fail to respond to their wishes; in particular, the narrow sectional interests of political parties and traditional interest groups have not engaged with new thinking and new needs.

The subsequent sense of alienation felt by many environmentalists has therefore led them to see direct action as a normal, acceptable and necessary mode of operation. Dobson sees it as a radical expression of this viewpoint, and notes the tendency to 'do-it-yourself politics; groups of (mostly) young people organise around a squat, a sound system, a drug, a piece of land and try to live a self-reliant life'. He regards their approach as a reaction to their 'disillusionment with mainstream political parties and [the] agendas they promote'.

Activists feel that their interests have not been fairly considered and that no-one in authority has read or listened to their case. They have gone through the usual democratic channels, or they may not have bothered. Direct action may seem to be the only worthwhile outlet available. Bureaucracy can be very slow to respond, and the temptation to force its hand is considerable.

Yet if everyone broke the law when they disliked some particular aspect of it, chaos would result. Law-breaking is a serious matter and should in a democracy be the course of last resort. Those who campaign on a law and order platform, especially on the political Right, will be particularly condemnatory of selective obedience to the law, in which people pick and choose the bits of it which they are prepared to accept. They will see this as a slippery slope which can have dangerous consequences, and are likely to disapprove of the activities of campaigners who are prepared to break the law to press their claims.

Many people on the Centre-Left would more easily accept that when those in authority are being totally unresponsive, direct action – even law-breaking – may be justifiable. They see it as being a most effective means of protest, for it has an advantage noted by Melchett:

> *Direct action doesn't just highlight issues; it simplifies highly complex subjects. It cuts through the jargon, mystery and bureaucracy, and it demands a straight answer.*

However, Martin has distinguished between the legitimacy of using peaceful direct action and violent protest. He finds the latter unacceptable for these reasons:

> *Violence as a means for obtaining social change has several flaws: it often causes suffering; it abdicates moral superiority and alienates potential support. It requires secrecy and hence leads to undemocratic decision-making; and, if successful, it tends to lead towards a violent and authoritarian new ruling elite. Non-violent action as a policy and as a technique avoids these problems; its means reflect its ends. With non-violent action, energy is aimed at policies or structures, and not their supporters.*

Wilson (*Pressure; The A-Z of Campaigning in Britain*) endorses this view whilst stressing that direct action should be used sparingly; the more it is used, the less effective it becomes. It should follow every possible effort to persuade by reason and reflect 'total frustration at the obstinacy, unfairness, and possibly the brutality of "the system"', rather than be a 'self-indulgent expression of the impatience of protesters.

History confirms that direct action often works, and many of the great social and political reforms owe something to the use of force, when aggrieved and obstinate people have manned the barricades – the extension of the vote in 1832, and the recognition of the female right to vote both followed such forms of campaigning. Today, ministers are aware of the strength of protest on issues such as new road schemes, and the review of the 'Dirty Dozen' planned by the Conservatives is an illustration that protest may contribute to a change of approach.

THE FATE OF BRITISH ENVIRONMENTAL PRESSURE GROUPS

According to *Social Trends* (vol. 24), the largest leading British environmental pressure groups in 1992 were the RSPCA, World Wide Fund for Nature, Greenpeace, FoE and Ramblers' Association. Like other cause groups, they tend to have a high turnover in their membership, and those who join in one year often fail to renew. What is clear, however, is that all of them have experienced a substantial explosion in membership over the two previous decades (see Table 3). Grant notes that the best-resourced British group has been the RSPB, and that this organisation 'was closely involved with the European Commission in the formulation of the EC Directive on the conservation of wild birds'.

Table 3: *The largest British environmental groups: membership*		
	1981	1995
National Trust	1,050,000	2,300,000
RSPB	440,000	890,000
Wildlife Trust	140,000	260,000
Greenpeace	30,000	410,000
FoE	18,000	230,000
World Wide Fund for Nature	60,000	210,000
Woodland Trust	20,000	150,000
Ramblers' Association	37,000	94,000
CPRE	29,000	45,000

SOURCE: ADAPTED FROM FIGURES QUOTED BY D. TOKE, *TALKING POLITICS*, VOL. 9:2

DIFFICULTIES OF GROUP CAMPAIGNING

If environmental groups enjoyed an upsurge in number and size in the 1970s and 1980s, they lost some ground in the early 1990s when the recession made its impact on interest in environmental issues. Several leading groups had to reduce their full-time staff and seek other economies. Apart from economic recession, another difficulty is the likelihood of schism. In some cases, their objectives are controversial, causing strife within the organisation. Environmental groups are prone to internal divisions over contentious matters of policy. Within the RSPCA, a section of the membership prefers to adopt a high profile and engage in direct campaigning, whereas others prefer to seek to influence those in authority by quieter discussion and consultation. Division also extends to individual policies as well as to the methods employed. Fox-hunting has been a difficult issue to handle. In the case of the National Trust, a number of its members both support and practise the sport, whereas others see this as an anti-social and unacceptable form of behaviour.

The Observer also discerned a sense of 'doom fatigue' among the public. It suggested that many voters wondered whether in spite of the greater prominence of environmental matters the interest really made much difference. Because of the lack of funds brought about by their reduced membership, some groups have been forced to concentrate on one issue, for many of them lacked the funding to pursue all the objectives which they would have liked to tackle.

Research carried out by Jordan et al (*Political Studies Association Paper, 1994*) indicates a high level of membership turnover among cause groups. Only 35 per cent of those who joined FoE in 1991 rejoined in 1992. Even so, the membership of environmental groups – particularly newer and more radical ones – has expanded rapidly over the last three decades, a period when party membership has been declining. Promotional groups may often be less favourably resourced than the protective variety, but even if they have less money, they benefit from the support of enthusiastic activists willing to devote time and energy to their cause.

CONCLUSION

McCormick (*Developments in British Politics*) notes that Britain has 'the oldest, strongest, best-organised and most widely supported environmental lobby in the world'. However, Robin Grove-White of the Centre for Environmental Change at Lancaster University sees the traditional environmental movement as changing:

There is a growing proliferation of new, frequently fragile, but vibrant social networks developing around issues like health, food, gender, personal growth, leisure, animals and vegetarianism.

He points to social changes such as the growth in the number of vegetarians to around some 2.5 million in Britain, and the fact that according to Gallup some 40 per cent of the population now eat less meat, and that this is even showing up in the electorally significant C1, C2 and D social groups where people are beginning to eschew meat-eating. Such trends reflect a new sensibility about responsibility and also a lack of trust in the processes of food production, but much of the concern comes from people who are not members of any group at all and who have nothing to do with the wider environmental movement as such.

There has been an historical shift away from the Victorian-style protection groups such as the RSPB and towards radical action, and a move from the conservation approach to a whole questioning of speciesism, indicating the way in which the green movement is moving towards a post-humanist agenda.

SUMMARY

MOVEMENTS

- *New social movements* challenge a dominant set of ideas and assumptions, and have a radical edge and visions of a world transformed; they are usually distinguished by their informal, decentralised and ultra-democratic forms of organisation. In Western Europe, the broad thrusts concern nature conservation, political ecology and the anti-nuclear movement.

ENVIRONMENTAL PRESSURE GROUPS

Various means of classification
- *Traditional protective (interest) groups and promotional (cause) groups.* The British Waste Paper Association and The Body Shop are primarily self-interested, but most environmental groups are cause ones, eg CPRE and FoE.
- *Insider or outsider?* (NFU and CPRE are insiders, Earth First! and Greenpeace outsiders).
- Or can be distinguished according to *area of activity*, eg those concerned with: wildlife protection – RSPB
protection of amenities – CPRE, Nimby
anti-road campaigning – Alarm UK
broadly-based national and international activity – Greenpeace.

Methods
- *RSPB*: insider status (consultations with Whitehall departments), MPs, media, Europe.
- *FoE*: more contacts with government than in early days (becoming an insider?), media, local groups (often involvement in direct-action protests, as well as coordination of Earth Action groups of young people), Europe.
- *Earth First!*: direct action, which can be violent.

Membership

- Large and growing, strong among young people. Increased involvement of middle classes, even in direct actions such as protests and demonstrations.

STUDY GUIDES

In your notes, you should ensure that you distinguish between movements and pressure groups, and understand the characteristics and modes of operation of new social movements.

For pressure groups, classify in the way you think most appropriate and convincing, and include relevant examples for each category. You need a section on the methods adopted to advance their position, showing which outlets are the most effective.

Ensure that you understand the importance of direct action and of Europe for environmental pressure groups. Indeed, environmental groups provide good examples for more general questions which examiners may use on the merits or otherwise of direct action.

Exam Hints

Questions on groups are likely to focus on three main areas:

1 General ones on membership, types, methods and factors influencing their success.
2 More specific ones (perhaps following a stimulus passage on the activities of one particular group).
3 The use of direct action by environmental groups. With what success?

Which environmental groups are most effective at popularising their cause and influencing governmental action?

Key words are 'effective', 'popularising' and 'influence'. You are being asked to make a judgement on the relative merits of the various groups. Several groups can be considered, and some are more effective than others. But of course we need to ask, 'Effective at what?' They may grab the headlines by eye-catching stunts. Does this necessarily enable them to achieve greater influence over government? Having pointed to some of the main groups, discuss their methods and comment on the strengths and limitations of their activities.

Group Work

There are several themes which could provide fertile ground for individual enquiries or lively class discussion. Each member of the group could be allocated one pressure group or movement to research, summarising its development, size, methods and success or otherwise before reporting back. This could lead to a discussion of the most effective tactics for environmental pressure groups and enable a view to emerge of the general factors which influence the fate of such organisations.

There are various possibilities for a debate in this area, topics such as animal rights and direct action being especially contentious. For instance, how about organising speeches on the motion that:

This house believes that violent direct action has no place in advancing the green agenda.

Practice Questions

1   Imagine that you are a member of FoE and the RSPCA and wish to advance the views of your association. What strategy and tactics might you adopt, and what kind of factors would determine the success or otherwise of your activities?
2   Compare the activities and tactics of environmental pressure groups with those of other types of pressure groups.

Glossary

Ecotage   Direct action in the environmental field, such as acts of sabotage on buildings and equipment; similar to eco-terrorism as already defined (see p 34).

Further Reading and Resources

Grant, W. (1995) *Pressure Groups, Politics and Democracy in Britain*, Harvester Wheatsheaf

Garner, R. (1993) *Animals, Politics and Morality*, MUP

Garner, R. (1994) *Environmental Politics*, Harvester Wheatsheaf

Lowe, P. and Goyder, J. (1983) *Environmental Groups in Politics*, Allen and Unwin

Mazey, S. and Richardson, J. 'Pressure Groups and the EC' *Politics Review*, September 1993

Watts, D. (1996) *Introducing the European Union*, Politics Association/SHU Press

4

GREEN POLITICAL PARTIES

Introduction

POLITICAL PARTIES ARE basic to the operation of Western liberal democratic systems. They are the primary method of selecting those who exercise political power and largely determine the content of electoral and legislative agendas. In addition, the parliamentary structure of most European governments converts party – or combination of party – majorities into control of the basic institutions of government; government in these systems is largely the result of party cooperation or confrontation between parties.

Several features of green parties serve to distinguish them from the mainstream parties which have dominated the political landscape in the developed world. They are often seen as part of the family of 'new politics' parties which tend to have a distinctive ideology, a participatory form of organisation, and a wide appeal among the younger, educated, concerned middle classes. They are sometimes referred to as Left-libertarian parties, a term which includes not only environmentalist parties but also some other organisations of the Left. They share similar ideological concerns, and again tend to be committed to decentralised power structures and to appeal to a similar audience. They are of course distinguished from other Left-libertarian groups because of their focus on ecological matters.

There are considerable variations among green parties. They adopt ideologies, forms of organisations and strategies which differ in significant details. Some writers portray these differences in terms of the light green/dark green distinction which we have already discussed on pp 18–20. Others use terms such as realist (realos) and fundamentalist (fundis), or electoralist and decentralist, but whichever classification is used the dispute is of a similar kind. It concerns the relationship of the parties to the theories of ecology and to the organisational structures which characterise new social movements. However, such distinctions over ideology and strategy are not of themselves sufficient to understand green party change and development in recent years. To understand the transformation within green parties, we need to examine their characteristics, patterns of conflict, and the structural and institutional processes which underlie their development. We must also examine the external political environment in which they operate.

Key Points

As you read this chapter, ask yourself:

- Why do some greens despair of party-political activity altogether?
- What factors have determined the success or otherwise of European green parties?
- Why has the Green Party in Germany achieved a measure of success, whereas progress by greens in the USA has been much more modest?
- Why are green parties so prone to schism?
- To what extent has the British Green Party made any significant impact on the British political scene?

GREEN APPROACHES TO PARTY CONFLICT

There are three basic ways in which environmentalists have responded to the electoral and party-based system of Western democracies. Some have tried to abstain from electoral politics altogether. Others have devoted their attention to influencing existing political parties in the hope that they might take on elements of their ideological approach. Finally, pragmatists have seen wisdom in seeking to create green parties. The greening of other parties is considered in the following chapter, and here we briefly consider the first option before concentrating on the third one.

THE REJECTION OF PARTY POLITICS

Many environmentalists believe that the game of party politics as played by the traditional players is incapable of resolving ecological problems. They portray party politicians as essentially self-interested power-seekers whose main preoccupation is to remain in power for as long as possible. To do this, they need to advance a party platform that offends as few voters as possible, and certainly they do not wish to alienate people in society who wield significant power. Not surprisingly, according to this view, they end up closely resembling each other, each striving to capture the same electoral support and fearful of antagonising key interests. Given such an approach to acquiring and retaining office, it is not surprising that established political parties fail to challenge the status quo when it comes to environmental problems, and that they fail to define and pursue green political goals. Hence they are largely uninterested in resolving difficult environmental problems.

Most environmentalists know that there is little chance that greens will be in government in the foreseeable future. So why participate in a game that they cannot win? If they become involved and support one party, there is a risk that they will create a backlash in which the 'wronged' party will become hostile to their concerns – an outcome which would endanger their wish to make interest in the environment a universal preoccupation. Furthermore, there is a belief that not only the goals but also the manner of playing traditional party politics goes against the grain of the new politics of environmentalism. A popular view among some French environmentalists runs as follows: 'Elections: piège a cons' (Elections: a trap for idiots).

SHUNNING THE PARTY-POLITICAL PROCESS

Martin has encouraged green thinkers to shun electoral politics, and suggests seven reasons for so doing:

1 Entering election campaigns reaffirms the value of existing structures rather than challenging the bureaucratic organisation of the state or the profit system.
2 Focusing on elections and seeking to woo politicians does little to establish the green movement as a viable force outside the parliamentary arena, a consequence being that once an exhausting campaign is over, the movement is enfeebled and virtually collapses.
3 The emphasis on personal responsibility for environmental problems is destroyed once people feel that the issues have been handed over to elected politicians.
4 The recognition that politicians are concerned to win and keep political power. Their wish for political survival and success makes it unlikely that they will confront powerful vested interests. Even the most sympathetic among them are still constrained by such pressures, and the tendency is to adopt compromise policies which maximise support even if these are actually anti-environmental in their effect. Above all, needing to win the next election, they are concerned with economic growth and its attainment, for this provides the key to various spending programmes they wish to put forward. They are not in a position to proffer anti-capitalist policies which would jeopardise business confidence.
5 By entering the electoral arena, environmentalists risk polarising opinion along party lines. Potential supporters of the environmental cause in the party not endorsed will be alienated and difficult to win round.
6 The environmental movement requires the participation of all its adherents if it is to maximise its following and achieve its objectives. By contrast, the

demands of election campaigning – with the media wishing to interview and emphasise the role of key personalities – require a concentration on the activities and performance of individuals at the helm, and an insistence on party unity and the avoidance of those splits which can occur when members speak their minds.

7 Opportunities within the political system other than those presented via electioneering are often ignored.

SOURCE: BASED ON B. MARTIN, 'ENVIRONMENTALISM AND ELECTORALISM', *THE ECOLOGIST*, VOL. 14:3

Martin's views reflect his interest in and emphasis on the Australian experience. Environmentalists in Australia have been especially reticent about party-political involvement, and were slow to develop their own green party. They have tended to concentrate on winning the hearts and minds of their fellow-countrypeople over the longer term rather than focus on the immediate political battleground. More radical members see current party politics as a distraction from their serious and difficult business, and in as much as they deal with the short term, are more interested in mobilising people for effective direct action. Others may already belong to existing political parties, and prefer to seek to persuade them to take up their concerns and incorporate them within party agendas; they see no reason to create new political parties.

GREEN-PARTY EXPERIMENTS

Green parties have been formed all over the world, often in response to the experience of new-social-movement politics or the lobbying practices of environmental NGOs. The first such party was formed in New Zealand in 1972, under the title of the Values Party. Several others have been created, and such parties are in the ascendant, particularly where their growth has been assisted by the use of a proportional electoral system. In the 1994 European elections, they received 10 per cent of the votes in Ireland and Luxembourg, and a little less in Austria and Finland. Even Taiwan has a green MP.

The experience of places such as Australia, Austria, France, Germany, Sweden, the USA and Britain is illustrative of the effectiveness or otherwise of many of the initiatives to create green parties. In each country, environmental movements have used different strategies to deal with electoral politics and have had different degrees of success. In the rest of this chapter, we will consider the contrasting experience of green parties and their basic characteristics, as well as some of the reasons for their relative success or failure. In so doing, we will concentrate on Britain, but draw extensively on the experience of the other countries listed.

Realists or pragmatists within the green movement in most countries have seen merit in contesting elections in the hope of achieving some wider political influence. In so deciding, they have been influenced by many factors, several of which are itemised below. The results are varied, as Table 4 indicates.

THE CASE FOR GREEN-PARTY ACTIVITY

With the exception of the German greens and the occasional state or local government party elsewhere, activists understand that their prospects of office, alone or in coalition, are rather small. So what is the point of trying to create and operate green political parties? There are some important advantages that can flow from involvement in electoral politics, and these include:

- The possibility (albeit a remote one) of gaining representation, even conceivably of holding the balance of power. This brings environmental issues into parliaments and local council chambers, draws attention to the cause and helps set the political agenda. The unusual prospect of achieving a balance-of-power situation may be tempting, for such a position enhances green influence in bargaining over which party holds office and what kinds of policies are introduced. Greens, Democrats and Independents have for some time occupied such a role in the Australian Senate. The same thing happened in the state of Tasmania (1989), where the Australian Labour Party could only form an administration by doing a deal with five green independents.
- The chance to win access to the media, for instance in Britain by putting up at least 50 candidates and thereby earning the entitlement to a Party Election Broadcast. Parties are likely to get their activities reported in Britain, as television functions under the requirements of balance laid down in the Representation of the People Act. As a consequence, there has been at least a partial increase in media coverage of environmental issues at election-time.
- The chance to show legitimacy, by being perceived as a player on the political scene. Environmentalists are now perceived as advocates of authentic day-to-day concerns, and are no longer regarded as cranky, peripheral or dangerously radical.
- The opportunity to spoil the prospects of another party, in the way that, by standing on a green ticket in California (the state with the most seats in the Electoral College), Ralph Nader felt he could damage the Democrats' chances of winning and also gain media coverage of green issues if enough disillusioned left-leaning voters deserted to him. Nader and fellow greens did not want to see a Republican in the White House, but he used his campaign as a lever to extract environmental concessions from President Bill Clinton. Following Nader's decision to run, the President became more active in environmental matters and spoke out against increased logging in public forests.
- The opportunity to assess both popular support and, of course, the strength of other parties which oppose green concerns.

- The chance to gain financial rewards by standing in elections. Costs are reimbursed in Germany, so that polling and political education can be conducted at public expense. Goldberg points to a different opportunity. The British Columbian Green Party has exploited the regulations concerning political contributions which are tax-deductible in Canada. It formed an Environmental Defenders' Fund using the slogan 'You pay $25 – Ottawa pays $75'. The money is used to support direct-action forest environmentalists and their families, by paying their fines and legal costs.
- The provision of a home for protest voters. In Britain they normally turn to a third party such as the Liberal Democrats when they wish to show dissatisfaction, particularly in local and Euro elections, and by-elections. In Ireland, Doyle and McEachern note that many citizens vote for Comhaontas Glas in both local and EU elections, support which evaporates in national elections.

Table 4: *Environmentalist parties in the EU*			
Average % Vote in National Elections, 1975–89			
Austria	5.0	Belgium	5.5
Denmark	0.9	France	3.0
Germany (West)	6.1	Greece	0.4
Ireland	1.1	Italy	3.3
Luxembourg	6.2	Netherlands	1.9
Spain	0.7	Britain	0.3

Source: adapted from I. Budge, K. Newton et al, *The Politics of the New Europe*, Longman, 1997

THE STATE OF GREEN PARTIES OVERSEAS

Australia

Green parties have existed in Australia since the formation of the United Tasmania Group in the late 1970s. They exist at the local, state and national levels. The national Australian Green Party was launched as late as 1992, its slow formation being caused by two main factors:

1 In a federal country, there were bitter arguments and intense rivalries between the national greens and smaller green parties in both South and Western Australia.
2 Also, there was a long-standing sentiment among many Australian environmentalists against participating in more mainstream political forums such as political parties.

There have been some recent successes on the Australian scene. Two green candidates won election to the Senate in the 1996 federal election, among them the Green Party leader who became famous because of his involvement in the Tasmanian Wilderness Society's successful bid to stop the building of the Franklin Dam in Tasmania's forests in 1983. In 1989, also in Tasmania, five green Independents were briefly in government after having created a Labour–Green Accord. During the mid-1990s, two Western Australian green senators sometimes held the balance of power in the national upper house, and used this position to bargain successfully with parties both in government and in opposition.

Austria

The Austrian greens, Vereinte Grune Osterreichs, have undergone several changes in recent years, notably in creating a more professional party, with a more tightly-controlled organisation which allowed them to be more effective on the political stage. As their party lost some of its seats in the Nationalrat, members recognised that they needed to develop policies over a broader area if issues if they were to be perceived as significant players; environmental issues have had less salience in Austria in recent years. As part of the reassessment of its ideological stance, the party has shifted from an anti-EU stance to a more sympathetic position, not least because of fear among supporters that hostility to the EU would place them in the same camp as the Freedom Party of the Far Right.

Germany

In January 1980, a diverse alliance of activists launched the national West German party, Die Grünen, or Greens; this was the first party to employ a name which later became almost universally adopted. Frankland notes that supporters 'agreed that the pillars of the new party would be grass-roots democracy, social concern, ecology and non-violence'. Early successes in the Landtage were built upon with representation in the Bundestag in the 1980s, which began in 1983 when the organisation polled 5.6 per cent of the national vote, converting into 27 green deputies. Four years later, this representation grew to 42 members.

In the early days, Die Grünen referred to itself as a 'movement-party', understanding that there were major advantages to be had if some of its social-movement characteristics could be retained. Partly as a result, even today the German greens have problems finding day-to-day operational activists, as many supporters insist on devoting large amounts of their time to extra-parliamentary activities. Much emphasis is still placed on the importance of lower-level units which are given substantial power to participate directly in high-level decisions. But by far the most famous example of the party's distinctive ideals is the 'rotation principle', which initially limited sitting MPs to two years in the Bundestag. This insistence on challenging the existing way of doing things led to many creative and sometimes destructive tensions within the party. Schisms continued throughout the 1980s, often depicted as a conflict between two opposing factions, the realos versus the fundis:

1 The realos argued that their programme of reform would have more chance of implementation if they played party politics by the existing rules and were willing to experiment with coalition politics involving alliances with the Social Democrats (SPD).

2 The fundis involved themselves in extra-parliamentary activities and supported more radical declarations.

By the end of the 1980s, Die Grünen began to lose momentum, in part because of the feuding between the two groups, but also because of the problems of reunification. Nationalism and other issues came to the fore, and Die Grünen polled poorly during the early 1990s.

However, since the coming together of the East and West German organisations in 1993, things have markedly improved. The greens polled 10.1 per cent of the national vote in the June 1994 European elections, giving them 12 seats in the Strasbourg Parliament. That progress was continued in the general election of October 1998, as a result of which the party was enabled to enter into a national coalition with the Social Democrats to provide Germany with its first major change of political direction for 16 years. Having obtained nearly 7 per cent of the popular vote and 47 seats, it was rewarded with three cabinet posts, leader Joschka Fischer becoming the country's Foreign Minister.

What has been most fascinating is this recent willingness of the membership to forge alliances with major parties (particularly the SPD), resulting in a share in government in some Länder (states) as well as in Bonn. The experience of governing inevitably creates new kinds of policy dilemmas for the greens, over which disagreement can emerge. However, their difficulties over the last decade are to some extent ones of success, for despite experiencing a period of self-doubt over the best strategies to be employed, Die Grünen has shown that it can win enough seats to be an active participant in both German and European electoral politics.

The radical style of Die Grünen and its approach to political life has in the past contrasted sharply with the 'normal politics' adopted by the country's conventional parties. It has 'grown-up', and whereas Fischer was an outsider who wore jeans and sneakers when he was first elected, today he is one of the top and most-respected parliamentary performers in the Bundestag and his party's most successful vote-winner. In the 1998 campaign, he transfixed his audiences by on the one hand portraying a horror vision of the future, whilst on the other reassuring them that they can still create a new, harmonious world of social justice and environmental responsibility.

Fischer claims that the principles of the party have not changed since those early radical days:

What has changed is that our basic strategic conflict has been decided: in favour of becoming a reforming party rather than pure opposition to the system.

Sweden

The Swedish green party, Mijopartiet, is less radical than its counterparts in several Western European countries, and as in the case of the Austrian greens, there has been a move towards greater professionalism and the development of a more all-embracing programme. For a while, it lost all representation in the Riksdag, as environmental issues moved off-stage. Again, some realignment was necessary, and new policy positions were adopted. In particular, the party did the opposite to the Austrian one and adopted a hostile stance towards the EU. This made it more distinctive, and may have contributed to its revival in recent elections.

USA

Of the four case studies listed, the US history of green electoral politics is the poorest. Several green parties have been formed at local and state levels. At the national level, the 'Green Politics Network' was formed at a conference in June 1995. According to Kagin (*Dissent*):

It seeks to group, under one spreading redwood, radical environmentalists and feminists, multi-cultural leftists, campaigners against the military budget, and that dwindling if hardy faction of citizens who still call themselves 'socialist'.

The Network helped to foster the move to run a candidate for the Presidency in 1996. Nader, the founder of the consumer movement in the USA, ran on a green party ticket in California. As we have ssen on page 62, the importance of the challenge may have pressured Democrat President Bill Clinton into advocating environmental causes more loudly.

In the USA green party highlights are hard to find, but there have been more numerous local victories. Few have been more enjoyed than those achieved by the New Mexico Green Party. In 1994, the greens landed a seat on the Santa Fé City Council. In a follow-up to this success, a nomination for the treasurership won a record-breaking 33 per cent of the vote, more than any third-party candidate to run for state office in the last 60 years.

BRITISH EXPERIENCE: THE EVOLUTION OF GREEN PARTIES

In Britain, there was initially a People Party, formed by a small group of activists from Coventry in 1973. Within two years it became the **Ecology Party**. According to Richardson and Rootes, the new body was at first dominated by the ideologically 'purer' ecologists (those who attributed intrinsic value to the earth) rather than by the environmentalists (those who simply cared for 'the betterment of human society'). As a single-issue party it lacked much appeal. Nonetheless in 1979 it published *The Real Alternative*, written by Porritt among others, a study which gives an indication of early green thinking. It called for six main moves towards:

1 A sustainable way of life, conserving the earth's capital and learning to rely mainly on those resources which can be renewed or recycled.
2 A stable economy, ensuring basic material security and prosperity for all.
3 Economic self-sufficiency in terms of the basic necessities of life, particularly food and energy.
4 A decentralised way of life, so that people become more responsible for themselves and others.
5 Seeing things in the long term rather than settling for convenient short-term measures.
6 A society which places less emphasis on material values, and more on personal development and achievement.

As the Ecology Party developed into the Green Party (1985), it widened its array of policies and campaigned on the whole spectrum of political issues. Supporters built up an image which had a simple appeal and seemed to be of growing relevance. For many people, it seemed self-evidently sensible to wish to save the ozone layer and the whale, and the emphasis on conservation rather than commercialisation was attractive to them. The chosen title, the Greens, neatly encapsulated their appeal in a single word.

It was the success of the Greens in the 1989 European elections which changed things, and forced politicians of all parties to take note of their arrival on the political stage. The result of the elections, in which the party won 14.9 per cent of the vote, appeared to indicate a new public interest in environmental matters. It may be that many of those who voted Green did so as an anti-government protest at a time when the third party (the newly-formed Liberal Democrats) was in its infancy and undergoing serious teething problems; yet nonetheless a succession of polls suggested that the public placed green issues high on their list of priorities. Margaret Thatcher, whose premiership had hitherto shown no significant commitment to environmental issues, was moved to describe the protection of the balance of nature as one of the 'great challenges of the late twentieth century'.

As the table indicates, the impressive 14.9 per cent yielded no seats in the European Parliament, an illustration of the difficulties of any minor party fighting under the First Past The Post (FPTP) electoral system:

Table 5: *Green Party results in 1989 European elections*			
	No. of seats	% Seats	% Votes
Britain	0	0.0	14.9
France	9	11.0	10.5
Germany	8	9.9	8.4

The Greens continued to do well in the local elections of the following year, but thereafter their political impact quickly diminished. They did much less well in the 1992 general election when they contested 253 seats. In the constituencies contested, their candidates gained an average share of the vote which was lower than it had been in 1987. On one occasion shortly afterwards, the party suffered the humiliation of being beaten in a by-election by the Monster Raving Loony Party! In 1997, only 95 candidates were fielded, and the vote received was a derisory 0.2 per cent.

Table 6: *Green-Party progress in elections since 1979 (% of overall vote)*			
GENERAL ELECTIONS		EUROPEAN ELECTIONS	
1979	0.1	1979	0.0
1983	0.2	1984	0.6
1987	0.3	1989	14.9
1992	0.5	1994	3.2
1997	0.2	1999	6.2

If the party lacked credibility in Westminster elections, it polled more strongly in the local ones of the early–mid-1990s, averaging around 5 per cent of the popular vote. In the Euro-elections of 1994, the Greens were unable to do anything like as well as on the previous occasion. Nowhere in England did their candidate do better than achieve fourth place. They managed to save three deposits, their best result coming from a prominent party spokesperson, Jean Lambert, who obtained 6.5 per cent in London North East. A breakthrough occurred in 1999 for, helped by the introduction of a proportionally electoral system, they secured two seats in the Strasbourg assembly.

The British Green Party history is a relatively long and chequered one, characterised by several internal schisms not unlike the more famous West German disputes between the fundamentalists and the realists. Rootes observes:

> *The dispute within the party is not about matters of environmental policy but about organisational structure. 'Realists' like Jonathon Porritt and Sarah Parkin assert that the party has squandered public sympathy by giving an impression of confusion and disorganisation, and argue for a formally elected leadership while 'fundamentalists' dislike talk of leadership as anathema, and argue for maximum decentralisation within the party.*

Today, the party has a representative in the new devolved Parliament in Edinburgh, as well as its two MEPs. Membership is much lower than in the peak year of 1989, but there are many local groups in existence around the country. The Greens have a strong profile in some towns, and gained 14 additional seats in the 1999 council elections. Most of their councillors sit on lower tier authorities. Those in rural areas tend to be more conservative than their urban compatriots.

Without reform of the electoral system for Westminster, green parties will probably remain peripheral in British politics. This probably accounts for the number of leading green figures who are active in Charter 88, the movement aiming for constitutional reform.

WHY DID THE GREENS LOSE THEIR ELECTORAL APPEAL IN THE 1990s?

Greens are now keen to portray the 1989 result as a freak one, the product of protest voting at a time when there was no other repository for such a vote. After all, the Liberal Democrats had just been formed as a result of a merger, and in their weakened condition were unable to attract their usual level of support. There was also unprecedented public concern about environmental problems in the light of Chernobyl and other such high-profile news items. Greens therefore suggest that there were far fewer committed supporters of their party at that time than the impressive voting figures indicated. They had done far better than could reasonably have been expected, and so they could shrug off later disappointments by claiming that the membership had become a more realistic one, comprising the 'true believers'.

It may be true that many voters were not really true greens at all, but there are other factors which account for their decline. Some of these fall within the responsibility of the party itself, for it was beset by internal difficulties and schism, its leadership being of variable quality. More significantly, the three main parties had each made some concessions to green thinking, so that for some of them a specifically green party (inevitably seen as a party primarily concerned with one issue) was not the only way to demonstrate support. Liberals had long claimed to be environmentally-friendly, and Labour and Conservatives were keen to show that red and green, and blue and green, could mix.

Political attention was distracted by other issues such as the break-up of the Soviet Union, the fall of communist domination in Eastern Europe, the Gulf War and the Maastricht debates on the future of Europe. These were major and immediate issues which diverted the attention of the chattering classes from environmental matters.

Perhaps above all, the most important factor in the electoral decline was the recession. Although people were still concerned about the environment, this could be seen as a luxurious preoccupation at a time when there were more basic issues affecting family life, such as the lack of a job or the fear of losing one, and negative equity in the housing market. It was easier to show a concern for the quality of life when there were plenty of signs of material abundance. At a time of insecurity, bread-and-butter issues took precedence.

PAST DISAPPOINTMENTS: FUTURE OPPORTUNITIES

After the 1989 successes, Green 2000 was set up in a bid to relaunch the party and increase its effectiveness. Supporters argued that greens needed to 'get real'. They pointed out that an increasingly personality-dominated media is only going to reflect the increasingly personality-dominated main political parties. What was needed was organisation, image and leadership.

The value of the Green 2000 initiative was questioned by dark greens who saw it as a concession to the traditional party battle which they abhorred. They argued that in a two-party system in which there is a sizeable third party, it was pointless to try and participate. At best they would attract a minute percentage of the vote, so it was perhaps better to stare into the political abyss, make a principled retreat and decide to stay outside a fundamentally flawed system. In the meantime they could seek to boost their membership and await a more favourable political climate.

Advocates of the Green 2000 campaign were victorious in the party battles of the 1990s, and they were able to set about the process of internal reform with a view to establishing the party as an important player on the political scene. They were unable to deliver the electoral results they would have liked to have seen, and at present there seems little likelihood that a breakthrough is within sight. Their hopes for the future may rest in part on the fortunes of the Blair government. If it fails to deliver the changes which many people want, then they will be looking for a different alternative. Disaffected Labourites and natural greenies within the electorate might then enable the Green Party to achieve greater success, particularly if future elections were conducted under a different voting system. The 1999 European poll indicates that the tide may be turning in their favour.

COMMON FACTORS AFFECTING THE FORTUNES OF GREEN PARTIES

FACTIONAL BATTLES

Some writers have seen the success or otherwise of green parties in terms of their ideological divisions. We have referred to the split between electoralists and fundamentalists, or more broadly, shallow and dark greens. Yet not always has a realignment of a party's ideological position been the result of factional dispute. The Swedish upheaval in the early 1990s was achieved without bitterness, and was more a reflection of the emergence of a majority view that a more centralised and effectively-led party was necessary for success. Neither was there much internal feuding in Austria, where Frankland (*Green Politics Three*) tells us that the reassessment was achieved without 'incriminations, resignations and splinters'. In both cases, reassessment of ideas and strategy have helped to improve the parties' electoral standing.

In Britain and France, internal disagreements have been deep-rooted, and took place at a time when the electoral outlook seemed less congenial. Disappointment with the outcome of the 1992 election in Britain helped to promote a re-evaluation of how the Greens, with limited resources, should approach the matter of fighting national elections, and also helped to intensify factional disputes. The party has only recently begun to recover from this period of internal upheaval.

For green parties, and others too, internal disagreements are unlikely to produce the desired outcome at election time. However, sometimes those disagreements have been the result of a poor performance, rather than a significant contributory factor to the disappointment.

THE DEGREE OF ENVIRONMENTAL AWARENESS

Obviously, there must be a reasonable level of environmental awareness in any given country if there is to be party success, though even this only indicates potential support to be mobilised for electoral purposes. In Denmark and the Netherlands where environmental consciousness has been consistently high and where the issue has featured strongly in political debate, there are only small and poorly-supported green parties. To a lesser degree, the same is true in Italy where electoral progress has been modest. However, in Belgium and France, where awareness of environmental issues is less marked, green parties have at times been relatively successful. In Eastern Europe, environmental concerns have often seemed to be something of luxury, and in those circumstances there has been little development of viable green parties.

The broad conclusion is that although environmental awareness is a necessary prerequisite, the level of consciousness alone does not promote effective green-party activity. Polls point to relatively high levels of environmental support in Australia, Britain, Germany and the USA, but each country has very different experiences with the development of green parties.

INSTITUTIONAL ARRANGEMENTS

In all of the other countries we have examined, it is easier for a new political party to stand for election than it is in the USA. In Britain a nominal deposit is required from would-be parliamentary candidates, but otherwise there is no restriction upon individuals offering themselves for election. Yet the Green Party has found it difficult to establish itself, for some of the reasons given on pp 68–69. Indeed, in several countries, aspects of the political system conspire to make it difficult, though not impossible, for new parties to take a place in the political arena. In the USA several factors discourage the formation and successful operation of third parties. For instance:

- The laws in most states place barriers in the way of third parties as they attempt to secure a place on the ballot; they require large numbers of signatures, whereas the Democratic and Republican parties are granted automatic access.
- The public funding of campaigns is much more generous for the two major parties. At a federal level, third-party presidential candidates receive money after the election, by which time substantial costs have been incurred, and then only if they have garnered more than 5 per cent of the total vote. Major party candidates, by contrast, get large election grants immediately upon nomination. A wealthy person (eg Ross Perot in 1992 and 1996) may successfully overcome this difficulty, but a less well-funded green political party has obvious difficulties.

The electoral system in national elections

The electoral system is the major institutional factor which dampens the prospects of British, French and US green-party prospects. All of these countries use majoritarian systems. In contrast, the relative success of the other European and – to a lesser extent – the Australian green parties results from a more favourable method of voting, based on more proportional voting of some kind. Furthermore, under the country's hybrid system, all Germany's members of the Bundestag have been elected by the second, 'additional' vote rather than in the first, constituency vote.

In the First-Past-The-Post (FPTP) or winner-takes-all system as used in Britain and the USA, it is simply necessary to get the largest number of votes cast in a constituency to win. There is no representation for those who secure second place, however well they perform. FPTP systems tend to produce majority governments, the successful parties gaining far more seats held in Parliament than their percentage of the popular vote merits. As a general rule, First-Past-The-Post works to entrench a two-party system, and it is rare for any third force to make a significant breakthrough. The Liberal Democrats have been able to gain a considerable measure of success in recent years, but smaller parties – unless they are highly concentrated like Plaid Cymru in Wales – make little headway. For the Green Party, with geographically dispersed support and limited funds, FPTP has been an issue in the internal debate of the party. Without it, some activists wondered if there was really any point in running candidates in the 1997 election.

In France, where the second ballot or double vote is employed, Les Verts have faced similar difficulties. Its position has at times been worsened by a split in the green vote, which further undermined the chances of gaining significant representation.

Australia employs a preferential system, the alternative vote, which is not much more favourable for minor parties. A winning candidate must receive an absolute majority of votes (50.1 per cent) in a single-member constituency. But few parties' candidates receive an absolute majority on the first count, particularly in a country such as Australia where every citizen must vote. So second preferences of the other candidates (working from the bottom up) are redistributed among the higher polling parties until one crosses the threshold. Under this system, the Greens do have a greater say, however indirectly, over who governs, via the manner in which they use their second preferences. Policy deals are forged between prospective parties realistically vying for government, and environmentalists can push for legislation favourable to their cause. Doyle and McEachern point out that the 1990 federal election was won by Labour, at least in part, on the basis of the flow of environmental preferences.

Schemes of proportional representation offer the best chance to small parties to achieve their goal of gaining representation, for they attempt to achieve a balance between the proportion of votes won and the number of seats gained in the legislature. The Australian Senate and the New Zealand lower house employ PR, and in Germany the two-vote system attempts to balance greater proportionality with the existence of constituency representation and stable government. In whatever variety, such systems provide the best chance of green political success. In Austria and Sweden, the use of list systems has been particularly helpful. It has served to encourage green-party participation in elections, and in both countries some green representation has been achieved. Not surprisingly, the outlook of supporters of the green cause in such countries, about what can be gained by working through the established political process, is more optimistic than that of Les Verts and the British greens. That may be about to change in Britain, now that the advantages of party lists for small parties have been clearly illustrated in the European elections.

The type of electoral system is the most important institutional factor dictating the existence and, to a large extent, the success of green parties in achieving representation in parliamentary systems. Rootes writes:

> *In general, in countries with federal constitutions and proportional representation electoral systems, the institutional matrix is much more favourable for the development and success of green parties, and for the development of mutually beneficial relationships between green parties and the environmental movement, than it is in centralised unitary states with majoritarian electoral systems.*

THE EXTERNAL POLITICAL ENVIRONMENT: THE RIGHT CONTEXT FOR SUCCESS

The existence of a high level of environmental awareness and a favourable electoral system do not alone guarantee electoral success. Circumstances, timing and even individual personality can matter. Parties are not isolated phenomena, and their identity and success can vary according to the prevailing economic, social and political environment in which they operate.

In a country or region where green concerns have to some degree been met by a greening of the established parties, there may be less scope for green parties to wave their alternative banner, whereas if there is no such response, the traditional mainstream parties may be vulnerable to any green electoral challenges. Yet often green electoral/political success has little to do with the meeting of environmental concerns, and other factors come into play. There may be internal turmoil within one of the other parties, for example, in the way that the Liberal Democrats, the normal repository for third-party protest voting in Britain, were undergoing the trauma associated with a merger in 1989. Again, economic factors such as the British recession of the early 1990s may hinder green progress, even if they also damaged the governing party.

All minor parties have to search for political space within the political system to enable them to establish a clear identity. In Sweden, for instance, space is congested by the existence of several parties, and – competing as they do with the Centre Party – the greens have adopted a relatively liberal and centrist stance, making them a less radical grouping than many of their fellows in Western Europe. In Britain and France, the fight for space has also been a problem. French politics are widely perceived in terms of an ideological cleavage of Left and Right, so that environmental issues do not easily fit into the party spectrum. In such a situation, some members of Les Verts are keen to gain representation in order to have an outlet for their views, but differ among themselves as to their ideological position. Others are more disillusioned with the political system, and doubt the value of pursuing the parliamentary route at all. Britain similarly provides little space for new parties, so that some activists seek to find a role beyond the party battle. They feel that their campaigning voice via pressure groups makes them more effective.

CONCLUSION

There are three possible electoral approaches for environmentalists to adopt:

1 They may take the path of the political outsider and deliberately abstain from party politics. Under this scenario, they concentrate on working for longer-term, perhaps more profound, changes in the future, possibly by working through a vigorous campaigning group.
2 There is the alternative of insider politics, by which campaigners seek to lobby and even work within the mainstream parties, hoping to win concessions such as policy changes. Such greening is discussed in the following chapter.
3 The final option is to form separate green political parties. This involves becoming part of the party system, though it does not mean that a green party has to operate in exactly the same way as the traditional parties which tend to be leader-dominated, centralised and hierarchical. Of course, even where the

decision has been taken to pursue the party political route, it is still possible for environmentalists to operate in a manner which recognises that the green party is just one useful feature of the wider environmental cause.

Different parts of the environmental movement in any country can work in different ways. Some are more appropriate than others at particular times, and the more forms of activity which exist, the greater the likelihood of achieving effective progress.

SUMMARY

Table 7: *The case for and against having separate green political parties; three arguments*

FOR	AGAINST
1 Chance to gain office or hold balance of power, and thereby achieve political influence.	Elected representatives are too prone to compromise and betray deep-green principles.
2 Opportunity to gain access to media, eg Party Election Broadcasts.	Electioneering too dependent on media requirement for personalities at expense of issues.
3 Chance to assess actual level of support and strength of opposition.	Prevents focus on establishing environmental movement as a force beyond parliamentary arena, to the neglect of other strategies.

GENERAL FACTORS DETERMINING THE SUCCESS OF GREEN PARTIES

- Level of unity, existence of factional battles.
- Level of environmental awareness in community.
- Institutional arrangements, such as type of electoral system.
- Nature of external political environment.

THE SUCCESS OF BRITISH GREENS

- 1989 Euro-election, the high peak of electoral success.
- Success in local elections around the country.
- Success in Scottish and European elections in 1999.
- Problems in the 1990s
  a Internal division.
  b Electoral system, FPTP.
  c Difficulty of finding space on political spectrum.
  d Emergence of other immediately-more-pressing issues.
  e Greening of other parties which have stolen some light-green clothing.

STUDY GUIDES

There are four main aspects to make notes on in your survey of green political parties:

1 The differing approaches of greens to political involvement.
2 The fate of green parties in Europe and beyond.
3 The evolution of the Green Party in Britain, its successes, failures, problems and significance.
4 Common factors affecting the success or otherwise of green parties, especially the importance of the electoral system.

Exam Hints

In any comparative paper on modern politics, information in 2 above could be helpful in answering a question on green parties or on third parties more generally. Otherwise the comparative material is useful in writing on the British Green Party, as a means of comparing alternative strategies, problems and successes. You might do well to choose one or possibly two countries on which you could write a paragraph or so, to give you a basis for such comparison.

Questions on environmental political parties tend to focus more on the problems of the Green Party following its success in the 1989 Euro-elections. They often concentrate on the problems the party has experienced in recent years, and this may be linked with the FPTP electoral system.

You may also be able to include material on the Green Party in a more general answer on third or minor parties, such as:

'Third Parties have made little headway in British Politics.' Discuss.

Of course the recent experience of the German greens could be relevant to any discussion of electoral systems and coalition governments, particularly on the merits and problems of coalition politics.

Group Work

Individuals or small groups can look at areas such as the German greens, the British greens, and green parties in Australia, and report back on their findings. This could lead to a discussion of the common factors in their success or failure, focusing on such considerations as strategies adopted, the electoral system and attitudes to party-political involvement. A group might debate the issue of green involvement in party politics, along the lines that:

This house believes that greens are more likely to achieve their objectives by working through pressure groups and direct action, rather than via traditional party politics.

Assuming that you or your colleagues were active in the British Green Party, how would you attempt to translate public concern about the environment into votes for your organisation? Make a list of a few ideas, and compare notes.

Practice Questions

1 Discuss the view that environmental issues are best handled through pressure groups rather than green political parties.
2 Account for the relative failure of the British Greens in the 1990s.

Further Reading

Doyle, T. and McEachern, D. (1998) *Environment and Politics*, Routledge
Garner, R. (1996) *Environmental Politics*, Harvester Wheatsheaf

5

THE GREENING OF EXISTING PARTIES AND GOVERNMENTS

Introduction

GOVERNMENTS TEND TO be slow to react to the activities of groups campaigning on new issues, and do so only when there seem to be compelling reasons for action. The typical response of ministers in several countries has been that:

- Many of the environmental dangers are as yet unproven.
- Much desirable action cannot be afforded.
- Neither industry nor the public are ready for seriously sacrificial action.
- Action to meet the various threats cannot but be piecemeal.

In many ways this reaction is not surprising. The concept of a major environmental threat is relatively new; the environmental degradation the world is experiencing is mostly gradual and undramatic, and democratic politicians tend to be preoccupied with immediate and short-term issues. Yet this does not excuse governments and political parties from planning for the long term. Many activities which may be desirable in combating environmental pollution, such as energy conservation, are worthwhile pursuing for their own sake. Policies needed to address these concerns will prove to be of value in tackling the eventual problems of resource depletion. The task of building economies and societies which are environmentally sustainable will therefore be one of the biggest challenges of the new century.

By the 1980s, environmental movements had made some progress in getting green issues placed onto the political agenda. Some of that response was merely to add a tinge of green to policies already in existence, often wrapping existing policy in a coating of fine rhetoric. In other cases more effort has been made to make environmental concern feature more strongly throughout the whole range of governmental thinking.

Key Points

As you read this chapter, ask yourself:

- Why did governments around the world begin to take green thinking on board in the 1980s and 1990s?
- Was it possible to be Conservative and to be green at the same time in the Thatcher/Major era?
- Why were green campaigners (a) satisfied and (b) dissatisfied with Tory policy?
- In what ways did the USA and Britain react differently to the green challenge?
- Has Labour yet shown significant signs of fulfilling the expectations of green lobbyists who had worked with it in the years of opposition?

THE SEARCH FOR SUSTAINABLE DEVELOPMENT

Some politicians across the globe have been committed to seeking ways of balancing environmental awareness with the pursuit of economic development. Their attempts were apparent in the debates of the UN Conference on Trade and Development (UNCTAD) and the Brandt Report on Third World development. At the Stockholm and Rio Earth Summits of 1972 and 1992 there was much discussion of the need to work towards a programme of sustainable development.

This concept had been tentatively outlined at the Stockholm Conference, but later it emerged in documents relating to national conservation strategies in Australia and the USA. It was amplified in the Brundtland Report *Our Common Future* and was later to become the subject of an initiative from the British government in 1994.

Sustainable development is based on the idea that it is necessary to ensure that there is a sufficient flow of natural resources in order to maintain economic production. There is a need for the soil to be able to sustain food production, and for an abundance of clean air, rivers and oceans to ensure the survival of animal and plant life. A slogan sometimes heard among those who speak the language of environmentalists is that:

---

sustainable development is development that meets the needs of today's generation while not impairing the needs of future generations.

Its fulfilment requires a recasting of much traditional thinking about policy-making and the considerations which influence the process. In the meantime, it is a convenient phrase much used by politicians who wish to parade their green credentials – if only as a strategy for staving off informed environmental criticism. In itself, it is not a radical-green concept, for the assumption underlying it is the primacy of economic growth and the need to ensure that the environment can be made to serve the human good.

In recent years governments and politicians have been forced to develop a more coherent framework for demonstrating their environmental credentials. Although there have not been many votes on the issue, the importance of green matters has been highlighted by other considerations – further scientific evidence about the danger of unregulated technological development, the greater power and sophistication of the environmentalist lobby and the impact of the EU (many of whose member states have been ahead of Britain in pressing environmental matters). Some have taken bold initiatives, whilst others have been content to dress up existing policy in environmentally-friendly language.

As yet, however, governments across the developed and developing world have been unwilling to place the environment at the core of their thinking on policy issues. They have tended to respond to particular problems which reach media attention, such as banning CFCs, saving the whale and creating game reserves. Policies adopted have not been allowed to imperil economic growth; their inspiration being cosmeticism or opportunism rather than deep-seated commitment to a changed set of values.

THE CASE OF AUSTRALIA

Doyle and McEachern quote the Hawke-led (Labour) governments in Australia (1983–91) as ones which attempted to make the concept of sustainable development meaningful. Until then the term had often been used by businesspeople who wanted to defend themselves from criticism of their lack of interest in matters environmental, but after 1983, ministers were willing to trade off environmental protection of specific sites for endorsement from environmental organisations at election time. Activists in the green cause were brought into the discussions of ecologically sustainable development programmes (ESD), an attempt was made to produce broad policy parameters for key sections of the economy, and reports were written to assess the extent to which ESD had been implemented. Electoral considerations may have been the inspiration for much of this activity, which was not always taken seriously in practice. But the example provides an illustration of the ways by which some politicians have attempted to accommodate themselves to environmental concerns.

THE EXPERIENCE OF THE USA

At first, the emphasis in the USA was on federal action, for it was felt that the states and local councils lacked the will to take necessary measures. Between 1960 and 1980, there were more than 25 federal enactments, and a particularly important measure was the establishment of the Environmental Protection Agency in 1972. Its brief was to coordinate protection initiatives and oversee their implementation. In the Carter Presidency (1977–81), several people sympathetic to the green cause were appointed to key offices.

Although the world oil crisis of the early 1970s showed the dangers associated with excessive use of energy by US citizens and, according to environmentalists, illustrated the need to curb excessive use, the recession which hit the Western world made many politicians realise the costs involved in regulatory activity. Anything which increased costs of production was unwelcome to industrialists, and some political leaders (particularly on the Right) began to dwell on the over-burdensome nature of environmental controls. In particular, they felt that higher taxation to finance regulation was a threat to entrepreneurial activity. Protection was seen as too expensive, rather than as a legislative priority.

As economic recovery got under way in the 1980s, the emphasis was upon promoting growth rather than controlling pollution, and the Republican administrations sought to reduce the extent of federal control. In the early Reagan years (1981–89), there was a real attempt to shift the responsibility for managing environmental policy to state and local level, the President being personally unsympathetic to regulatory federal policies. He believed that the country could not afford the costs of environmental protection. He preferred to allow private interests to have their way, and in pursuit of his deregulatory initiatives, he 'packed' the Environmental Protection Agency with staff who shared his outlook, and cut both the budget and personnel.

In the Bush years (1989–93), there was a gap between rhetoric and reality. Even though he claimed to be the 'environmentalist President', leading figures in the White House were uneasy about the stringent controls required by the Clean Air Act of 1990. He worked with the green lobby in the preparation of the measure, but the regulatory framework it provided proved to be a rather weaker one than supporters of the legislation would have wished.

Renewed importance had been attached to the role of the states during the Reagan era. Accordingly, it was necessary for groups to organise around the country rather than rely on influence in Washington. In several states, branches of existing pressure groups were formed, whereas in others new associations took up the cause. Lobbying over the environment at this level became more important to the environmental movement, and some state administrations showed a sense of urgency in taking up new initiatives. New York was vigorous in its attempt to solve problems of impurities in the water supply; California pioneered air pollution control (especially of emission systems), and New Jersey was in the forefront of programmes to handle toxic waste matter – it was also the first state to adopt mandatory recycling laws. The states were the testing-ground for experimentation, and others began to take up measures as the need for regulation became evident.

Of the main political parties, the Democrats are more sympathetic to environmental regulation. In some areas such as the western states, environmentalists are a key component of the groups making up the Democratic Party, and in several of them, legislators standing on the party ticket show a much greater concern for issues of conservation and anti-pollution. In 1992, the Clinton platform was again overtly pro-environment, and the Vice-Presidential nominee, Al Gore, was an active spokesperson for the cause. Environmentalists were keen to support the Democrats, and indeed for several years many of them had involved themselves in candidate selection. Such involvement of the green groups within the party caused internal problems, for it created expectations which proved difficult to satisfy.

There were high expectations for the Clinton administration, the more so as several people with green interests were appointed to high office. Sometimes, these expectations have not been fulfilled. Francis, writing on environmental policy (*Developments in American Policy*), quotes the example of grazing fees. The President had proposed to increase these for grazing animals on public lands, a move popular with the environmentalists who felt that the ranchers (mainly large corporations rather than old-style pioneers) of the West were subsidised by the taxpayer in that they were allowed to graze stock on lands adjacent to their own at below the market rate. Furthermore, the practice was seen as ecologically unsound for it was damaging to the fragile landscape of the region. Opponents of the attempt to raise fees saw the tradition as a well-established one and rejected any interference with existing rights; they portrayed this as a serious inroad into the Western way of life.

If the President had carried out his policy, it would have pleased the green lobby and brought in a useful source of revenue. Yet, when it ran into serious opposition and Western senators made it clear that they would not support the budget if proposals for increased fees were retained, Clinton backed down. He later did a deal with a Congressional coalition which resulted in a modest doubling of what were anyway very low rates, and did not press this when Western senators filibustered the proposal.

In the USA, Davies and Waldstein (*Political Issues in America*) have noted that there has not been the same commitment to environmental action as that which characterises the more enterprising states of the EU. They note the lack of a clear idea on what it means to be green and the attitude of many manufacturers such as the President of Dupont and others, who declare themselves to be of a 'green complexion'. There is 'some sense of shared vision, but little sense of how to attain it'.

ENVIRONMENTAL POLICY IN BRITAIN: GOVERNMENT ACTION ON THE ENVIRONMENT

Environmental policy was not an innovation of the last two decades. It has a longer history than this, and the existence of many campaigning groups and several statutes are evidence of this gradual evolution. In areas such as air quality and land use, action had been taken well before 1979. However, before we examine the initiatives taken by various governments, it is useful to be clear about what we understand by environmental policy and who is responsible for it.

THE NATURE OF ENVIRONMENTAL POLICY

McCormick has written about the meaning and scope of environmental policy. He suggests that, in an ideal world, economic and social development would be not only productive and profitable, but also sustainable. He limits his definition in this way: 'Environmental policy concerns itself with the relationship between people and their natural environment.' The definition would appear to exclude consideration of urban policy which is difficult to include under the category of 'natural environment', and fails to distinguish itself very much from rural social policy in general.

Blowers (*Public Administration*, vol. 65:3) was more prescriptive in his definition, and focused narrowly on 'the use of land and the regulation of human activities which have an impact on our physical surroundings'. This does not exclude urban matters, but the use of the term 'regulation' places the emphasis on the need for those in power to strive for a balanced use of land, recognising the demands of development, conservation and ecology. The emphasis on regulation possibly omits inclusion of the wider debate about public policy, resulting as it does from the activities of campaigning groups and other interested bodies.

In essence, environmental policy is concerned with what Lowe and Flynn see as:

an accretion of common law, statutes, agencies, procedures and policies. There is no environmental policy other than the sum of these individual elements, most of which have been pragmatic and incremental responses to specific problems and the evolution of relevant scientific knowledge.

British ministers have been slow to accept that the environment is a distinctive area of policy. It tends to be viewed as a bolt-on extra, and as such it can be sacrificed when other demands seem to be more immediate and pressing. This is why developments have amounted to what Braybrooke and Lindblom (*A Strategy of Decision*) refer to as 'disjointed incrementalism'. On the one hand, there have been bold advances such as the Clean Air Act (see p 93) and the creation of the Department of the Environment (DoE), yet there has been no broad strategy. Britain has relied heavily on 'ad hocism', and until recently little attention has been paid to creating what McCormick calls 'a rational institutional and legislative structure'. The result is that 'it is difficult to say exactly who is responsible for making and implementing environmental policy in Britain'.

Before proceeding to look at national developments involving the introduction of new governmental machinery, it is worth pointing out that local government has a significant role in implementing environmental policy. Many tasks of regulation have been given to councils, and this includes the responsibilities imposed by the various Public Health Acts, Clean Air Acts, Control of Pollution Acts and the Environmental Protection Act of 1990.

THE CREATION OF THE DEPARTMENT OF THE ENVIRONMENT

In 1970 a new DoE was created by the Heath government in order to bring under one roof some of the responsibilities which had an environmental impact. This was one of the super-ministries then in vogue, and its purpose was explained in a White Paper on *The Reorganisation of Central Government*:

> *It is increasingly accepted that maintaining a decent environment, improving people's living conditions and providing for adequate transport facilities, all come together in the planning of development ... Because these functions interact, and because they give rise to acute and conflicting requirements, a new form of organisation is needed at the centre of the administrative system.*

Of course, such administrative reorganisation was no substitute for an environmental policy, a topic on which Edward Heath had expounded when still in opposition (April 1970):

> *decisions [on the machinery of government] do not ... amount to a policy ... The environment is by definition inter-disciplinary and all-embracing. Almost all departments are involved. Almost all proposals for action have an environmental as well as an economic cost ... we are used to looking at the latter, but not the former.*

In the four years which followed, it became apparent that the creation of the new department did not amount to a serious attempt to put the environment at centre-stage. The powers allocated to ministers were insufficiently wide-ranging, and key decisions were taken elsewhere in Whitehall. Agrarian and countryside matters remained with the Ministry of Agriculture, and the development of policy on energy was made the responsibility of another new department. Within two years of the fall of the Heath administration, transport also had been removed from the DoE.

PARTY APPROACHES IN BRITAIN SINCE 1979

From the 1980s onwards, all of the main political parties in Britain became increasingly interested in the environment. In 1979 the manifestos had dismissed environmental issues in brief references, and Margaret Thatcher shortly afterwards described them as 'humdrum'. The Liberals showed more concern than the other two, and their anti-nuclear-power position and interest in community politics indicated a concern lacking elsewhere. However, even within the Liberal Party, it was the rank-and-file rather than the leadership which displayed a genuine zeal, and after the formation of the Alliance with the Social Democrats in 1983, the radicalism of traditional Liberal policy either disappeared or was concealed from view. Some of it has re-emerged in the more recent guise of the Liberal Democrat Party.

Environmentalism was more prominent on the agenda in 1983 than it had been four years earlier, but as Robinson notes, the 'token' declarations were there to 'look good', and actually meant very little. Thereafter, however, the greening of the parties acquired some momentum, and Garner draws attention to the increasing number of conference resolutions and party publications on the issue. He notes that Labour's environmental proposals were well-received by the pressure-group activists. The Party was suggesting the creation of a new Ministry of Environmental Protection, legislation on the protection of the countryside and wildlife, and new controls to cover air and water pollution.

The Conservative response, 1979–90

The Conservatives were back in office in 1979. Given that they were dominated by the formidable figure of Margaret Thatcher, the leader's approach to environmental matters was crucial. She had often given the impression of hostility rather than lack of interest. Flynn and Lowe (*Green Politics Two*) draw attention to a Cabinet leak of the early 1980s which conveyed the importance of reducing 'over-sensitivity to environmental considerations'. Yet by the end of the decade, her mind had been changed, a rare example of a Thatcherite U-turn. She addressed the Royal Society in 1988, and spoke of the importance of sustainable development and of the need to nurture the environment. A year later, the Party Conference heard that the Conservatives were 'not merely friends of the Earth' but also 'its guardians and trustees for generations to come'. Her new-found commitment and the actions which followed gave the topic a greater priority in government thinking and helped to promote a response from the other parties.

Her conversion and the increased interest of other parties reflected to some degree the pressure of external opinion, as environmental matters became the theme of media discussion; activists were interviewed and featured in various political programmes. However, some have traced her change of heart further back to the mid-1980s when it was apparent that greens were doing well in

European elections, particularly in Germany, and there was the possibility of their acquiring a higher profile at home.

There were perhaps other motives besides party expediency. Maybe she wished to enhance her position as a global statesperson. The environmental issue would serve to raise her profile by suggesting a concern for issues over and above the immediate party battle. Maybe she had simply become aware of the severity of environmental problems and of the need for action. Certainly within her own party there were many people in the 1980s who became concerned that Britain's heritage was in danger from what Garner calls 'the ravages of urban expansion'. Their preoccupation with the green belt reflected a wider concern for the preservation of the countryside. Indeed, a party pamphlet went so far as to claim that: 'The nature conservationist is a natural conservative.' However, the Conservatives who promoted such arguments were usually the 'wet' paternalists rather than the neo-liberals whose attitudes she generally shared.

Whatever the motive, the Thatcher government did begin to display a greater enthusiasm for taking action. A White Paper produced in 1990, *This Common Inheritance* (see below, p 87), illustrated the new awareness. So too did the appointment of Chris Patten as Environment Secretary in 1989, for he has widely been viewed as one of the 'greenest' cabinet ministers of recent years. There were also factions within Labour and the other parties which echoed the green interest, and in the House of Commons there was often cross-party support for animal welfare, and conservation causes and legislation.

Yet for all of the greater interest, the responses of politicians in the Thatcher years did not amount to a convincing strategy. Thatcher's reactions were an example of the 'green tinge' variety of thinking. Presented with evidence of the serious problem of pollution in the North Sea and of the consequences which might derive from this, she felt inspired to commit her administration to incorporate environmental thinking into the policy-making procedures of her administration. She proposed national goals and wanted regular reports on the extent to which targets were being attained. Much media attention was devoted to this new departure in governmental policy, and for a while afterwards her statements were accompanied by fine rhetorical flourishes about the need for everyone to recognise the desirability – indeed the necessity – of exhibiting greater interest in environmental matters.

The Prime Minister picked up litter, and her party often portrayed green politics as synonymous with conservation, heritage and English values. There were, and are, genuine moderate environmentalists within the ranks of the Conservative Party. To most observers, the Prime Minister – the only political leader in living memory who refused to board a train – was not among them. Deep greens were scathing at the way in which the Thatcher government could live with leaky atomic submarines, cracked nuclear power stations, new motorways and a thriving arms-export industry.

'This Common Inheritance'

The publication of the 1990 White Paper marked the first attempt by British ministers to develop a comprehensive environmental policy. As such, it was a landmark of a kind. The document listed more than 350 measures, many of which were already being undertaken, plus suggestions for new legislation and other initiatives. Attention was drawn to the need for new machinery to handle issues such as energy efficiency, policies to cater for the protection of the countryside and a programme to combat nuisances such as noise pollution. The emphasis was on what was already being done rather than on innovatory ideas. It was widely reported that Patten's idea of a carbon tax was omitted because of pressure from development-oriented interests.

The response of the environmentalists was dismissive. They saw the publication as a lost opportunity to draw serious attention to environmental issues, and generally found the new proposals unimaginative and excessively timid. *The Times* noted 'the lowly status long accorded the issue of environmental protection in the government department normally entrusted with its care', and suggested that this resulted from the preoccupation of civil servants with issues of housing and local government on which they were more informed. *The Independent* of the same day was more unkind, its leader column referring to the White Paper as being 'as feeble as it is lengthy'. What was lacking was a coherent strategy for action, for although the White Paper urged policy coordination across departments, there was more rhetoric than commitment to effective and speedy action.

The Major Administrations 1990–97

John Major made his first key speech on the environment in 1991, and argued that 'the integrity and indivisibility of the environment should now be reflected in a unified agency'. He favoured a new and large centralised agency for 'environment protection and enhancement' to integrate the functions then handled by several other organisations. Such an institution had long been recommended by the permanent Royal Commission on Environmental Pollution, and a unified body was duly established five years later. The Environment Agency covers functions such as flood defence, water-resource management, pollution, control, conservation and fishery stocks. It is very different in kind from any of the much smaller agencies to which particular environmental problems have been delegated in the past.

As Environment Secretary, John Gummer was keen to display the government's green credentials. An organic farmer himself, he soon earned respect from many green lobbyists for his initiatives, several of which were welcomed by the opposition parties. He:

- introduced the legislation setting up the Environment Agency;
- helped to persuade the Chancellor to phase out leaded petrol;
- stressed the government's determination to meet pollution targets set in 1992 by the Rio Conference on global warming;

- issued planning guidance that opposed new out-of-town shopping centres;
- announced air quality targets for eight key pollutants.

Gummer recognised that roads were a major source of environmental pollution, but the nature of Conservative support made it difficult for him to act boldly to challenge reliance on the motor car. He was reluctant to impose targets for reducing road traffic and increased public provision, and over the controversial Newbury bypass scheme, he expressed his support for the route which would cut through open countryside and pose a threat to wildlife.

However, of all his activities, it was his 1994 statement on sustainable development which created the greatest interest among green activists.

Sustainable development: the case of the Major Administration
'Is your journey really necessary?' asked a poster issued by the Ministry of Information during the Second World War. The implication was that by curbing non-essential use of resources, everyone could 'do their bit' for Britain's war effort. In January 1994 Gummer appeared to strike a similar note when he launched a package of British government initiatives on environment policy. He indicated how the key concept of sustainable development would be presented at 'grass-roots level' through a new Citizen's Environment Initiative:

Everyone involved has to say 'Could I walk instead of drive, could I turn the lights off rather than leave them on, could I turn my central heating down a notch?'

The Times, 26.1.94

At that launch the British government published four documents as a 'coordinated follow up' to the agreements reached at the Earth Summit in Rio de Janeiro two years earlier. These were:

1 *Climate Change: The UK Programme*
2 *Biodiversity: The UK Action Plan*
3 *Sustainable Forestry: The UK Programme*
4 *Sustainable Development: The UK Strategy*

In placing the sustainable development strategy at the heart of its thinking and approach, the government made much of how widely it had consulted about its content. The DoE wrote to about 180 organisations and individuals, inviting comments on the scope and content of the strategy. A seminar was organised in Oxford in March 1993 involving about 100 organisations and individuals from all parts of Britain, to encourage further debate. In the final document, ministers launched three new initiatives for continuing to widen consultation about the sustainable-development agenda within Britain. These were:

1 A five-person *Panel of Experts*
2 A consultative *Round Table*
3 The *Citizen's Environment Initiative*

The minister's stance was not universally welcomed by green campaigners. Some felt that his fervour might help to bring environmental issues to the centre of policy-making, but others pointed out that where they had expected a lead from government, this renewed emphasis on individual action was a disappointment. Public environmental concern had mushroomed in most industrial societies without encouragement from governments. Many green campaigners believed that what was now urgently required was a strong lead in implementing solutions. As Sara Parkin, then one of the trio of leaders of the Green Party, later pointed out:

> Since Baroness Thatcher discovered the existence of the global environment as a political issue in 1988, green pressure groups, policy institutes and individual environmentalists have been consulted at great length by the Department of the Environment ... So it was no wonder that hearts sank when the consultation paper for this latest mega-document was circulated last year. It read as if nobody in the DoE had ever read anything sent in by any environmental group.
>
> *The Independent*, 26.1.94

Expectations had been raised but not fulfilled. Green groups were disappointed but not surprised by the content of the final text. What particularly dismayed them was that it contained none of the new commitments or policy initiatives which they had recommended. Feeling that their advice and hard work had been ignored, many green campaigners saw the launch as an opportunity missed. As Parkin went on to say, this conclusion was enhanced by unfavourable comparison with what had been achieved in other countries:

> The much-heralded documents on global warming, sustainable development, biodiversity and forests contain little more than a rearrangement of previous policy, with no indication that the Government has looked at the experience of either Germany or, better still, the Netherlands. While the Dutch National Environment Policy Plan, published in Spring 1989, may not satisfy the greenest of the green, it is one of the best around and it does contain what the UK one does not: targets and timetables, as well as mechanisms for monitoring and measuring progress.

Porritt pointed out the dangers for environmental groups if they agreed to further consultations without clear guidelines for implementing their proposals:

> Environmental organisations have a genuine grievance that there has been no substantiation of targets and timetables. Without those, in all honesty, it is possible to imagine a sequence of these meetings stretching from here to eternity without delivering the goods.
>
> *The Times*, 21.6.94

The need for what Major called 'a conversation across all sectors of society' was a recurring theme in governmental presentation of the strategy, and was the justification for establishing a round-table consultative process. Yet pressure groups had to ask themselves: what was the worth of all the contacts assiduously cultivated behind the scenes and in the consultation process, if the 'new' approach from ministers amounted to nothing more than an invitation to further talks?

Exploring the limits of greening policy within existing power structures has divided strong green movements elsewhere, particularly in Germany. As Rawcliffe suggested in a 1993 paper, the question of 'natural limits' to greening policy within prevailing power structures is unavoidable for environmental pressure groups, because it is 'through existing power structures that environmental pressure is both expressed and constrained'. Thus there is both danger and opportunity in moving closer to the existing centres of power. The balance between these is always a matter of judgement.

Labour in opposition: the 1997 Election

Labour's interest in green questions was slow to develop, its general indifference in the mid-1980s reflecting the lack of interest shown by the leader and the potential of the issue for internal party disagreement. Many Labour activists saw the environment as an issue of concern mainly to middle-class people who wished to preserve their rural way of life. They felt that it had little to do with the working class. Others saw the topic as one which threatened much-needed economic development and expansion. Such factors, combined with the attitudes of some leading figures, meant that Labour's commitment was at best sporadic.

In 1990 the party produced its first major statement on the environment, *An Earthly Chance*. It won the backing of many green individuals and groups, and was seen as more far-reaching than the recently-released Conservative White Paper. Not surprisingly, its proposals suggested a larger role for the state than Tory ministers were willing to accept, and it offered clear commitments on institutional reform and the control of noxious emissions. However, at a time of recession in the early 1990s, economic growth seemed to be a higher priority than the environment. Not surprisingly, the commitments in 1992 were not as bold or far-reaching as greens would have liked to have seen.

Labour now claims to be committed to the green cause. Before the 1997 election, it drafted a strong statement on the environment, arguably the strongest policy ever produced by a mainstream political party. In *Trust For Tomorrow*, it called for a cut in greenhouse gas emissions to 20 per cent below 1990 levels by the year 2010, twice the reduction proposed by the outgoing administration. Its 1997 manifesto put the issue:

at the heart of policy-making, so that it is not an add-on extra, but informs the whole of government, from housing and energy policy through to global warming and international agreements.

Every government department was to be a green department, for all of them 'must promote policies to sustain the environment'. The goal was to combine environmental sustainability with economic and social progress, and policies on areas such as transport were viewed as having a particularly important role in creating this desirable target.

In addition the 1997 manifesto wrote of the need to work through the European machinery to tackle issues on a wider scale. In particular, reform of the CAP was seen as a priority, for apart from its other deficiencies, the policy was not geared to environmental protection. Indeed, a new environmental internationalism was promised, with efforts made to push such matters higher up the agenda in discussions between world governments.

Labour in power 1997–?

Labour retains a commitment to some policies which – in the eyes of ecologists – dent its claims to be greener than its opponents. Nuclear weapons, increased economic growth and a traditional enthusiasm for the 'white-hot heat of the technological revolution' are all at variance with deep-green preoccupations. Nonetheless, some of the early work in office has pleased moderate environmentalists, although there are areas of disappointment. There was a general welcome for the inclusion of transport within the DoE, and a recognition that the new 'super-ministry' might be better equipped to handle environmental issues and sustainable development in a more integrated way. Also, it was noted that each major government department was given a 'green minister' who was to look after the environmental dimension when policy was being made.

The House of Commons Environmental Audit Committee report, published towards the end of Labour's first year, pointed to the need for action on green taxation. Green enthusiasts were also keen to see moves towards a greener budget, with the emphasis on moving taxation away from placing its burden on economic 'goods' such as labour, towards environmental 'bads' such as energy, pollution, transport and waste. Many of these proposals are already integrated into European tax systems, so that in Austria, France and Italy there are higher taxes for cars with more powerful engines; in Denmark there exists a waste tax which has dramatically encouraged recycling, and in Sweden a pesticide charge helps the country reach its goal of a sharp reduction of use.

The 1998 budget was the first to include an assessment of how the measures would impact on the environment. It marked a more concerted attack on car use, and included the provision of an extra £500 million for public transport – much of it to go to rural communities which had seriously inadequate bus services. Other measures included an increase in the landfill tax introduced by the Conservatives and an increase in fuel duties above the rate of inflation, with continuing encouragement for lower-sulphur diesel.

Action has been taken to change policy on the dumping of chemicals and nuclear waste at sea, removing from Britain the tag of the 'dirty man of Europe'. For the first time for two decades, Britain is in line with the rest of Europe on disposal of oil rigs, nuclear submarines and a range of toxic materials. The 'dilute and disperse' policy of the Conservatives has been abandoned, and ministers are cooperating with other European nations in a bid to eliminate pollution from the North Sea.

John Prescott, the Deputy Prime Minister who heads the Department of the Environment, Transport and the Regions, has declared that 60 per cent of new housing should be built on 'brown field' sites – renovated urban land – although many amenity groups are outraged that some incursions into the green belt have been approved. He has also produced a transport White Paper, the first for 25 years, outlining the most radical changes in policy since motorways were invented. The thrust is to tax congestion through toll and company car-park charges, diverting the proceeds into public transport. The overall intention is to persuade one in ten users to give up their vehicles, and the rest of us to use buses and trains more often. The practical rather than dramatic proposals have won the broad approval of the pressure group Transport 2000.

Other ideas are in the air, and one which is advocated by the Select Committee is an attempt to redefine the meaning of economic growth. Currently measured by gross domestic product (GDP), it charts the quantity of growth, but gives no guide to quality. The Index of Sustainable Welfare would enable ministers to achieve their stated goal of stable and economically sustainable growth.

For all the flurry of announcements, some members of the green lobby are still highly critical of parts of the Blair government's programme. They claim that enticing promises were made in opposition and at the election to keep the greens 'on board', and that these have been watered-down or ignored ever since.

ENVIRONMENTAL MACHINERY IN BRITAIN, 1999: A SUMMARY

- *DoE*: the political head is the Deputy Prime Minister, who is served by other ministers. The Department has responsibility for transport policy, which in the past has at times been separated off into a distinct ministry.
- *Environment Agency*: this has key responsibilities for flood defence, water-resource management, pollution control, fisheries, navigation, recreation and conservation.
- *Conservation agencies*: these include English Nature, English Heritage, the Countryside Commission and the Countryside Council for Wales.
- *Local authorities*: these have an important role in planning, enabling them to control the physical environment through determining land use, the construction and removal of buildings, road developments, the green belt etc.

In addition the *EU* has taken much interest in matters such as pollution control, the problems of waste (especially of the toxic variety), the conservation of finite resources such as fossil fuels, and the protection of flora and fauna. The EU lays down directives in these and other areas, as we explore in greater detail on pp 100–2.

KEY LEGISLATION ON THE ENVIRONMENT

Of the several statutes enacted by British ministers which have concerned the environment, the following are among the most important:

The Clean Air Act 1956

Introduced in the days before the environmental movement had taken off, the Act was aimed at resolving the problem of dense urban smog in London and other large centres of population. Smokeless zones were established, the burning of domestic coal was controlled, and emissions and grit were regulated. This was a significant step towards ending serious air pollution. A further act on the subject was passed in 1968 to tighten regulations.

The Control of Pollution Act 1974

An early measure to deal with various forms of pollution in the atmosphere, including noise pollution.

The Wildlife and Countryside Act 1981

One of the most important conservation measures since the war, the Act gave the Secretary of State wide-ranging powers to determine which species are to be granted protection. It was introduced without any significant consultation with relevant lobbying groups other than the RSPB.

The Water Act 1990

The statute which controversially privatised the water authorities also included provision for a National Rivers Authority, which was to be given responsibilities in areas such as control of floods, water resources and fishing rights, as well as duties in connection with pollution. Some of these tasks were later handed over to the Environment Agency.

The Environmental Protection Act 1990

An all-embracing measure of some 120 clauses, the Act was more comprehensive than anything which had been introduced previously in Britain. A significant innovation was the principle of integrated pollution control (IPC), by which ministers were to take steps to try and prevent pollution at source, and where practicable 'make the polluter pay'. The need to control all types of environmental pollution such as emissions of smoke, dust, grit and odour, was emphasised.

Much of the direct control over environmental matters falls on local authorities. It is county, metropolitan and district councils which are empowered or required to take action under much of the national legislation above. For instance, the 1990 measure obliged local authorities to develop strategies for recycling waste material, a target of 25 per cent being set for them to achieve by the year 2000.

SMOG IN LONDON

CONCLUSION

In Britain the three parties are all keen to claim that they are environment-friendly, and they have sought to develop what they see as coherent strategies for tackling key issues. They have begun to give serious consideration to matters such as resource-planning, recycling and the idea of sustainability, and in itself such progress is useful and very worthwhile. However, in the eyes of environmentalists, be they moderate or radical, the policies adopted fall short of what is required. Lobbyists are pleased to note the greater priority attached to issues such as pollution and the release of harmful emissions, but they see much of the legislation as tentative, open to evasion and aimed primarily at reassuring the voters that something is being done. In this regard, action taken has been mainly palliative and remedial rather than far-reaching and fundamental. They favour radical action involving a change of lifestyle, whereas the policies of successive governments have been based on the assumption that the pursuit of economic growth is of such cardinal importance that it cannot be cast aside. Only growth can provide the increased resources which will enhance living standards and finance more generous social provision.

This is a fundamental difference of approach. As Robinson puts it:

[The] main political parties are still chained to the idea that the natural eco-system exists primarily as a resource for man's exploitation … the sacred cow of economic growth has not been sacrificed, nor is it likely to be in the near future.

SUMMARY

- Governments are often slow to react to the arrival of green issues on to the political agenda. *Why?*
- The electorate expects to see greater provision of services or lower taxation, and these require economic growth. The deep-green message which questions the value/desirability of growth is therefore unpalatable.

But

- The green influence can, on occasion, be important to the fate of governments – eg Germany.
- A strong electoral performance and convincing evidence of the gravity of green issues can affect the attitudes of traditional parties which are in or out of office.

Table 8: *British parties and green issues*		
CONSERVATIVE	LABOUR	LIB DEM
• Thatcher moved to take up cause; pressure of electoral success at home and abroad. • Mounting evidence of environmental damage. • Difficulty of reconciling New Right policies with level of intervention necessary to protect environment. • Publication of *This Common Inheritance*. • Action under Major; Gummer approach, and 1994 White Paper. • 1996 Environment Agency.	• Indifferent for much of 1980s, potential area for disagreement. • Seen by some as middle-class conservationist issue; union attitudes could be hostile, eg workers in nuclear industry. • Publication of *An Earthly Chance*. • Stronger commitment in 1992. • Blair and New Labour pledge to place environment at heart of policy-making. • Early doubts of some green activists, but progress re transport etc.	• Liberal Party long more pro-environment than other parties. • Lib-Dem constitution commits party to safeguarding environment. • Policy statements often detailed and wide-ranging. • Lost initiative to Green Party in 1989; Greens replaced Lib Dems as a vehicle for protest voting, temporarily.

STUDY GUIDES

Revision Hints

In your notes you need to have sections on the approaches of the three main parties to environmental issues. You should be in a position to explain their growing awareness of environmental issues, and to assess what the Conservatives and Labour have done in office about them. Note also the various institutions and levels of government at which environmental issues are handled.

Exam Hints

The greening of parties and ministers is a possible question on any examination paper. Try to put yourself into the position of being able to make useful comparisons with the actions of governments elsewhere, eg Germany and the USA. See how different parties and politicians reacted to the growing environmental challenge, and what factors impeded some of them from taking up green issues with greater conviction and enthusiasm.

Group Work

Individuals could research the attitudes to, and the record on, green issues exhibited by the three main parties. Note any publications and relevant factors such as the importance of the union element in the Labour Party. It might assist you if you look at the election manifestos of the established parties in 1992 and 1997, and list any differences in the commitments given. The class can then discuss whether it is better to leave green issues to green parties, or whether they are best taken on board by existing parties. Is there a distinction between the possibility of taking up light-green issues, on the one hand, and that of taking up dark-green issues on the other?

Practice Questions

1 What do you consider to be the main influences affecting British environmental policy in the 1980s and 1990s?
2 Analyse and assess the main problems which environmental politics raise for actual and would-be ministers.
3 In what respects and to what extent have green issues been taken up by the established political parties in Britain?

Further Reading

Doyle, T. and McEachern, D. (1998) *Environment and Politics*, Routledge
Garner, R. (1996) *Environmental Politics*, Harvester Wheatsheaf
McCormick, J. (1998) *Developments in British Politics*, Macmillan
Pilkington, C. (1998) *Issues in British Politics*, Macmillan

6

THE GLOBAL DIMENSION

Introduction

POLLUTION AND ENVIRONMENTAL degradation do not recognise the borders of any one country, and in the continental land mass, national hazards can inevitably spill over into another state. It is because pollution knows no frontiers that environmental problems are best tackled in concert with other countries via international agreements.

The impact of environmental issues has already had a significant effect on the international system. Some of the nationalist movements in the Soviet Union that eventually swept away the world's most powerful Communist Party had their origins in the ecological protests of the early 1980s and before. Armed conflicts over scarce resources such as oil, and movements of populations away from land blighted by environmental disasters are becoming more and more common throughout the world.

The international community – as well as individual governments – finds the concept of a major environmental threat difficult to handle. The environmental degradation the world is experiencing is mostly gradual and undramatic, and democratic politicians tend to be preoccupied with immediate and short-term issues. It is, unfortunately, unlikely that this state of mind will change significantly until some major environmental catastrophe – such as the impact of global warming – has affected the developed world. This does not excuse governments and political parties from planning for the long term. The task of building economies and societies which are environmentally sustainable will therefore be one of the biggest challenges of the new century.

Key Points

As you read this chapter, ask yourself:

- In what respects did the Rio gathering mark a new departure in environmental thinking and action?
- Why was the EU slow to develop policies on the environment?
- Why is environmental policy an appropriate area for action by the EU?
- What are the main difficulties faced by the EU in developing an effective environmental policy?
- Why has Britain come into conflict with the EU over some aspects of environmental policy?

THE EARTH SUMMIT, RIO 1992

A crucial indicator of contemporary environmental policy-making lay in the UN Conference on Environment and Development (UNCED), or 'Earth Summit', held in Brazil in June 1992. Nine months before it started, the Director of the UN Environment Programme (UNEP) claimed that 'people everywhere look to 1992 as our last chance to save the Earth'. By this bench-mark, the Summit must be considered a failure. The agreements signed at Rio achieved little by way of the creation of an environmentally sustainable world. But by more modest standards, Rio offered some hope for the future.

The agreements themselves – treaties on biodiversity and on climate change; a set of principles for sustainable forestry; agreement on the need for a future convention on desertification; and *Agenda 21*, the blueprint for action to lead development into environmentally sustainable areas – are of relatively little value since either they are not legally binding or they lack timetables and cash commitments. Furthermore, in the eyes of some critics, the Summit failed to make an adequate link between the issues of poverty and population on the one hand, and environmental degradation on the other. With the significant exception of Japan, most donor countries continued to fudge their long-standing commitment to raising official development assistance to 0.7 per cent of GNP: there was no joint commitment to reducing levels of developing-country debt: all attempts to discuss trade and the operation of the GATT (now the World Trade Organisation) were rebuffed. The entire topic of population growth was largely kept off the agenda, mainly thanks to pressure from the Vatican and Catholic nations.

The planet was not to be 'saved' any more than it had been after the last UN conference on the environment, in Stockholm in 1972. But just as that conference left a legacy of environment ministries and legislation that helped the developed nations to improve their environments, so Rio's success would depend largely on the strength of the institutional machinery that it left behind. And in this respect the picture was not all gloomy.

The creation of the UN Sustainable Development Commission was the centrepiece of the institutional legacy of the Summit. Although there was no compulsion for states to submit, to the Commission, annual reports of their progress on the documents of intent signed at Rio, there would be strong pressure to do so, particularly on the larger countries. The above Commission was modelled on the UN Commission on Human Rights, and it was hoped that it would follow that body's record of getting results by embarrassing governments on the world stage. The climate-change treaty, with its obligations on signatories to draw up plans to stabilise their output of global warming gases, potentially placed a powerful weapon in the hands of national environmental lobbies.

Another institutional legacy was the growing importance of the Global Environment Facility, the source of funds for environmental projects that countries could not address on their own. The World Bank has subsequently emerged as the manager of most of the money pledged to the Facility (the UN Development Programme would manage one-third), and it is committed to ending funding for environmentally-damaging projects. The Facility will probably pay for the implementation of the two treaties and also any future ones which may be agreed; in general it should encourage international aid to become more environmentally sensitive.

The final bequest of Rio would be its influence on the attitudes of those who took part in it. Heads of state, businesspeople and journalists were forced to concentrate on environmental issues for several weeks, and commitments were given not only to current declarations but also to future action, with plans for further conferences, conventions and forums for discussion. (A hopeful analogy was the Montreal Convention, established in 1987 to limit CFC emissions. Although the original treaty was relatively weak, within three years the phase-out targets had been brought forward 10 years, and by 1996, CFCs were to be outlawed completely.)

Prior to Rio, there had been some concern about Britain's environmental performance. Preparations for the gathering appeared to be half-hearted, and the British record of signing up for initiatives had hardly indicated genuine interest. However, Prime Minister Major played a prominent role in the discussions and signed the biodiversity and global warming treaties on behalf of the British people. He also pledged £100 million of additional money intended to help address global environmental problems.

The action which Britain now takes on environmental matters is crucially affected by international agreements. The most recent report on sustainable development, *This Common Inheritance: UK Annual Report 1997*, described progress made in 1996 towards meeting some 650 commitments specified in earlier reports and in the original 1994 strategy document (see p 89). It also set out priorities for 1997, covering areas such as the National Air Quality Strategy, increasing international protection of the oceans, fish stocks and other marine resources, and the provision of improved information for consumers about products they purchase.

British policy on environmental protection is also much influenced by membership of the EU, to which we now turn.

THE EUROPEAN DIMENSION

The EU has been active in seeking to raise environmental standards among its members for many years, and some of the more recent entrants such as Austria and Sweden have always emphasised environmental concerns.

The Founding Treaties made no mention of environmental protection as a Community responsibility, primarily because the threat to the environment was not readily apparent in the 1950s. At the *Paris Summit in 1972*, EC leaders declared protection of the environment and the consumer to be pressing concerns, and called for an action programme. The Commission began thereafter to devise a series of detailed programmes and policies which have subsequently been developed and expanded.

The key initiative was the inclusion of this area of policy within the *Single European Act (SEA)* in 1986. Part of the process of harmonisation, needed to create the single market, necessitated setting higher environmental standards across the Community. A main principle of the evolving EC policy ever since then has been the adoption of preventive measures, so that in the devising and implementation of all policies, potential pollution and environmental damage have to be taken into account. The Environmental Compatibility Test (ECT) is now applied to public and private projects which have a substantial effect on the environment, such as the construction of motorways, refuse disposal plants and thermal power stations.

At Maastricht (December 1991), there was agreement on the following objectives of environmental policy to:

- Preserve, protect and improve the quality of the environment.
- Protect human health.
- Make prudent and rational use of natural resources.
- Promote international measures to deal with regional or world-wide environmental problems.

The objectives were deliberately couched in vague terminology, for this enabled them to command broad assent. However, their inclusion was an indication that the environment was now seen as an area of growing importance. It was widely accepted as desirable that it should be so recognised, for the environment is very much a Community affair. After all, acid rain poisons lakes and forests hundreds of miles from its sources, so that the air pollution created in Britain causes environmental damage in Northern Europe, just as any pollution in the upper Rhine is likely to affect France and Netherlands as well as Germany.

Where there is pollution in the EU, the 'polluter pays' principle is applied wherever possible so that those who cause the problem are liable to bear the costs of prevention, cleaning up and compensation for pollution, thereby providing manufacturers and others with the incentive not to pollute at all, to reduce pollution or to seek alternative and cleaner technologies. The EU wishes to encourage the manufacture of products less damaging to the environment, and firms are invited to apply for the EU eco-label. This may be awarded if the manufacture of a particular product does not consume too much energy or raw material, or result in toxic emissions into the air, soil or water, or generate too much noise or waste. The incentive is to produce clean, low-risk and sustainable technologies. In Britain, eco-labels have been awarded to Hoover for washing machines in the 'New Wave' range, and for such things as kitchen towels, toilet paper and paints.

CURRENT ACTION

Between 1973 and 1992, the Community established five Action Programmes on a wide array of subjects, and the fifth one of these covers the period through until the millennium. All have been based on the assumption that Community involvement was only desirable where the objectives it embraced could be better fulfilled at the EC level rather than by member states acting on their own.

Amongst the issues on which the EU legislates are water pollution (including setting standards for drinking-water), noise pollution, the packaging of chemicals and other products, and the transport and disposal of waste.

The fifth Action Programme, *Towards Sustainability*, is the boldest to date. It stresses the causes of pollution and identifies five areas where a strong EU approach is essential (agriculture, energy, industry, tourism and transport). The focus is on the way in which all EU policies must be made to conform to the needs of environmental policy, and on the differing responsibilities of all tiers of government, from local to European, in ensuring that appropriate action is taken.

The EU, covering as it does some 3 million or more square kilometres, is well-placed to tackle some of the most pressing environmental problems. Directives have been issued on matters ranging from the release of sulphur dioxide (1980) and lead in exhausts (1982), to the more recent one on habitat protection (1992) which was intended to ensure that flora and fauna are preserved or restored in any construction or other projects which may cause damage to wildlife. The Union has also given a lead in raising standards in areas such as water pollution, which Britain has been slower than some other countries to follow.

Scandinavia has long been at the forefront of attempts to tackle acid rain and other issues, and Denmark, a member for more than 20 years, has shown that action by national government can be effective. Some of the environmental groups in Denmark and Sweden have shown concern that in the drive towards the single market – with its emphasis on free competition – their high standards might be jeopardised.

Table 9: *High environmental standards in the EU*			
	AUSTRIA	SWEDEN	NORWAY
Control of heavy traffic	✓	✓	✓
Control of marketing of dangerous substances	✓	✓	✓
Labelling and classifying dangerous substances	✓	✓	✓
Control of substances which deplete ozone layer	✓	✓	✓
Action on dangerous waste	✓	✓	✓
Action on lead in petrol/exhaust fumes	✓	✓	✓
Use of economic regulators over environmental hazards	✓	✓	✓
Strict control over use of pesticides		✓	✓

SOURCE: ADAPTED FROM *CRISIS OR OPPORTUNITY? ENVIRONMENTAL POLICY*, P. BARNES, JEAN MONNET PAPERS, HUMBERSIDE UNIVERSITY, 1996

SOME PROBLEMS OF EU ENVIRONMENTAL POLICY

Although the EU recognises its responsibilities and may be seen as a suitable body to tackle environmental concerns, there are difficulties:

- Environmental policy still lacks the priority attached to achieving free competition. The creation of the single market has been the number one priority, and high environmental standards must not be allowed to lead to a distortion of trade by states making their own regulations as a subtle means of keeping out the goods of another state. In the chemical and packaging industries, some states have introduced tough rules as a means of protecting home industries.

   Moreover, in any conflict between protecting the environment and the needs of the market, it is often the wishes of the producers which carry the heavier weight. The Italians originally had an energy-efficient approach to the use of petrol, for the high cost of oil (all of which was imported) made it desirable to encourage the use of smaller cars. Yet pressure from the Commission, itself under the influence of the motor manufacturers, has led to a dilution of the original standards.

- Standards of implementation have varied among member states, partly because national pressures can undermine policy. Some countries have therefore managed to avoid the obligations laid upon them. In particular, domestic pressure from manufacturers and financial constraints have often limited the extent to which directives have been adopted. It can be very costly to comply with the standards laid down by the Commission, which is one reason why the 1975 directive on the quality of bathing water has been so half-heartedly implemented in several countries.

- In the past, it has always been easy for those who wish to evade their responsibilities to argue that the Rome Treaty did not establish environmental goals and that therefore there was no clear point of reference against which policies could be tested. This has enabled the laggard countries to comply only half-heartedly or not at all with EC initiatives. But at least the SEA made it clear that environmental policy was a legitimate area for Community concern, and it laid down minimum standards in several fields.

- Again, tackling unemployment in the Union at a time when some 20 million people are out of work is another major concern, and environmental policy cannot be a barrier to job creation. The tendency is for states to seek to achieve prosperity first rather than see environmental policy as integral to economic development.

- Even the most environmentally conscious in the EU (the Nordic states and Austria) are subject to pressures to adjust their priorities, for reasons of economic necessity. They are still a potential force for good in the Union, although, as less populous states, their influence on decisions is relatively small-scale, and this will reduce their ability to raise overall standards. Moreover, Norway, one of the pace-setters in environmental regulation, voted to stay outside the EU.

- The new democracies of Central and Eastern Europe are likely to have particular difficulty in meeting EU requirements, for some of them have been the victims of degradation during the years of Soviet domination when there was a concentration on intensive industrial development. Some states (eg Poland and Slovakia) used brown coal as the main energy supply, and this is a heavy pollutant. Also, existing legislation is often inadequately enforced.

THE PROBLEMS OF THE NORTH SEA

The state of the North Sea poses a particularly serious problem, and the International Council for the Exploration of the Sea (ICES), the official scientific advisers, foresees a catastrophic crash in some fish stocks without a serious attempt to tackle the linked problems of sea and air pollution. To protect species, action is needed on heavy metal, chemical and sewage pollution, and also on nutrient inputs – mostly fertiliser from farmland, and nitrates and phosphates from sewage works. Four hundred oil and gas installations and toxics spilled from oil tankers have added to the severity of the difficulties. Discharges from nuclear-fuel reprocessing plants – especially Sellafield and La Hague – at one time added to the problems, although these have been markedly reduced in recent years.

The problems of the North Sea are a microcosm of a looming global crisis of pollution and over-fishing. Whereas, according to the UN Food and Agriculture Organisation, all the world's major fishing grounds are now at or beyond their biological limits, the EU countries have over the years increased their subsidies to fishing fleets, with much of the money going into building larger boats. The Union has a policy of buying for scrap 20 per cent of Europe's fishing fleet to attack overfishing, yet it has provided hundreds of millions of pounds to aid poorer countries in building bigger boats.

If Europe cannot save the North Sea, there is little hope for other seas, for the EU has the most sophisticated system of regulation of trade and waste. In theory, it has a mechanism for controlling quotas and the size of fishing fleets. It has technical expertise, less corruption and more control in its fishing and waste industries than anywhere else in the world.

BRITAIN AND EUROPEAN ENVIRONMENTAL POLICY

British membership of the EC coincided with the era in which environmental politics began to interest the Community's policy-makers. As the Community became more active in establishing standards, British ministers found themselves forced to respond to initiatives from the Commission. Hence, in Milton's phrase (*Journal of Law and Society*, vol. 18):

> *the most striking feature of the Government's policy on pollution is the extent to which it is dictated by EC directives.*

It is EU directives which have forced the British government to tackle issues such as motor vehicle emissions, lead poisoning and other forms of air pollution resulting from, amongst other things, the dangers to the atmosphere presented by smoke and sulphur dioxide. Similarly, it is EU law which has placed questions of water quality and acid pollution onto the political agenda.

For years, it was common for British people to mock continental countries over the allegedly poor quality of their drinking water and the lack of hygiene in their sanitation arrangements. Yet as comparisons were increasingly made between British procedures and those of other member states in the Community, it became apparent that several of them had tighter standards of control than those operating in Britain.

The EU has introduced nearly 30 directives on the quality of water, affecting matters ranging from the low standards of sea-bathing water and the lack of cleanliness of beaches, to the impurities to be found in water for human consumption. British ministers responsible for water privatisation in the late 1980s found it necessary to establish the National Rivers Authority as a watchdog with powers to check pollution levels in lakes and rivers. As McCormick explains:

In short, EC law was able to achieve what many years of domestic and foreign pressure on the British Government had failed to achieve. This created an interesting irony; while the water industry was privatised (and thus freed of direct government control), it was also made subject to considerably stronger environmental regulation.

The same concern for high standards meant that in 1991 the Commission insisted that seven major construction projects be halted because there had been no assessment of their environmental impact. This failing was in direct contravention of a 1985 directive, and led the Commissioner, Carlo di Meana, to take legal action through the EC machinery over two of them. One of the seven concerned the building of the M3 across Twyford Down, an area of natural beauty and scientific interest near Winchester, but on this one the Commission was later persuaded to drop its objections.

TWYFORD DOWN, BEFORE THE ARRIVAL OF THE M3

There have been many complaints within the Union about Britain's performance on environmental policy – 125 in 1990. This may reflect the awareness and vigilance of the green lobby in Britain as well as inadequate compliance with directives in some areas. Overall, in 1991, Britain was the fourth most compliant nation among the 12 nations of the Community, its 23 offences being markedly better than Greece's 50 or Spain's 66.

The way ahead

There are new policies which could be adopted. They go beyond simply setting minimum standards, and include the development of a comprehensive strategy to link environmental concerns with economic and industrial policy. In particular, help for the countries of Central and Eastern Europe is necessary to assist these countries in overcoming the toxic legacy of the Soviet era and in improving their overall environmental standards.

The EU, given its size, location and composition, is in many ways an appropriate body to take action and urge the adoption of new policies. It provides the political forum within which the member countries can agree on common action to protect our shared environment. It has the potential to take the lead in the formulation and implementation of a global strategy to confront the ecological threat to the planet.

However, success depends on the political will to act, and this in turn depends upon the attitudes of 15 governments. Policy on the environment is one of those areas affected by the subsidiarity debate, and since the Edinburgh Council (December 1992), there has been pressure from some states to scale down EU involvement in national decision-making. Britain is not the only country to regard any reversal of previous trends with some relief, for the record of some of the Mediterranean states in environmental matters leaves much to be desired.

CONCLUSION

In the future, the environment is an area likely to grow in importance. If ever there was a topic on which it is necessary for governments to cooperate with each other, it is matters concerned with the well-being of the world we all inhabit. No aspect of the quality of life is more fundamental than the purity of the air we breathe and the water we drink. Pollution respects no national boundaries, and no state can preserve its environment by a strategy of isolationism. Many of the problems are not national but international. Action is often necessary on a larger scale and needs to take the form of a coordinated response. The Chernobyl disaster was but one indication of the way in which the internal problems of one state impinge seriously on many more. So too are the difficulties associated with acid rain and the threat to the ozone layer.

Whether or not the legacy of the Rio summit and other initiatives proves successful in the long term has yet to be seen. If nothing else, this legacy has served to remind peoples and politicians around the world of the global dimension we have surveyed. The point was similarly made clear at the Dublin meeting of the European Council in mid-1990, which was primarily concerned with European Community approaches:

The environment is dependent on our collective actions; tomorrow's environment depends on how we act today.

SUMMARY

ACTION AT THE INTERNATIONAL LEVEL

- 1972 UN Conference on the Environment, Stockholm.
- 1992 UN Earth Summit at Rio: *Agenda 21* and the need for sustainable development.
- International agencies include the UN Environment Programme (UNEP), the International Union for the Conservation of Nature (IUCN) and the EU.
- UNEP's work is primarily concerned with monitoring and assessing global issues; it lists 152 multilateral environmental agreements made up until 1990, and has also stressed the links between the environment and development. The IUCN incorporates government agencies and NGOs. Lacking executive powers, its reports are nonetheless widely respected.

ACTION BY THE EU

- 1972 Paris Summit: declaration in favour of protection of environment.
- 1986 Single European Act: acceptance of need for higher environmental standards across Community.
- 1991 Maastricht Treaty: agreement on a set of broad environmental goals.
- 1973–92 Five EC Action Programmes: fifth one entitled *Towards Sustainability* (1993–2000).

BRITAIN AND THE GLOBAL DIMENSION

The action Britain takes in the environmental field is in part dictated by agreements reached with other countries, a recognition of the fact that key issues can often only be tackled internationally. In spite of its reputation, the British record of compliance with EU directives is better than that of several other countries. However, it has had to be brought into line over issues such as the quality of water supplies and beaches, and acid rain emissions.

STUDY GUIDES

Revision Hints

In your notes, it would be wise to list the main machinery and agreements in which Britain is involved. However, it is the EU and its impact on environmental policy which is particularly important. You should have a record of the evolution of EC/EU initiatives, and be aware of the main advantages and problems of the Union in resolving environmental issues. If you are studying the EU as a main Paper Two option, then it is important to ensure that your coverage is more extensive.

Exam Hints

Candidates studying the EU are likely to be asked a whole question on environmental policy, and the EU's success or otherwise in tackling it. On Issues options for Paper Two, it is important to know how the European and global machinery have an impact on the development of British policy, and to have a record of any areas of dispute between Britain and the Union.

Group Work

Group discussion might concentrate on why the EU is a suitable body to deal with environmental issues, and particularly on whether key decisions on policy are better taken in London or in Brussels. Is this an area for subsidiarity, or one in which it is reasonable to accept that there are considerations which extend beyond national boundaries?

Practice Questions

1   Why has the EU become increasingly involved in environmental issues? What factors limit its effectiveness in this area?
2   Is environmental policy better handled at the European level, or should it be a matter for individual nation states?

Further Reading

Garner, R. (1996) *Environmental Politics*, Harvester Wheatsheaf
Young, S. 'Environmental Politics and the EC', *Politics Review*, February 1993

7

PAST DEVELOPMENTS, FUTURE POSSIBILITIES

Introduction

TODAY THE ENVIRONMENT is an area of mounting concern across the world, and people in many countries are involved in action to preserve wildlife, combat pollution and demand higher environmental standards across the board. A green ideology has been developed, weaving together many concerns ranging from animal rights to conservation, and millions have involved themselves in green pressure-groups and political parties. Further evidence of this widespread interest is the scale of interest in and attendance at conferences such as that held in Rio and elsewhere. In the circumstances, it was inevitable that politicians of conventional political parties would assume a hitherto-undiscovered commitment to saving the planet. The greening of politics is now well under way, and as Rudig (*Green Politics One*) suggests, green politics are here to stay:

> *They are not just going to fade away so long as serious environmental problems remain unsolved. More profoundly, they are arguably not simply issues any more; they reflect a more fundamental conflict which is concerned with the very nature of the future development of society as a whole.*

In the eyes of ecologists, there is an alternative to the present path taken by governments throughout the world. The deep-green perspective involves not merely finding answers to particular problems. Rather, it provides a framework for understanding the human and social predicament, the implementation of which would involve a fundamental change of life-style.

POLITICAL ACTION

Greens protest against various aspects of the present political system. Because of their disdain for the way it functions, there is an ambivalence in their attempts to promote their concerns via the established political channels. Some are willing to come to terms with a system they dislike, and seek to achieve their goals from the inside, but others – particularly those of a deeper shade of green – find this approach at best unattractive, but also probably ineffectual.

Many greens engaged in a variety of environmental, anti-nuclear and peace movements as part of the wave of protest which swept the 1970s. Finding that this did not give them significant political influence – in spite of the mobilisation of millions of people – they began to develop their own parties. Many of these were 'anti-party' parties, in that their mode of operation was distinct from more conventional and established ones. They were movement parties, coordinating bodies attuned to their grass roots. Their agenda was determined by the issues and by activists on the ground, rather than by some elitist leadership which laid down the party line.

'Neither Right, nor Left but up-front' in Porritt's words, they rejected the actual ideological spectrum. In their view, all other parties presupposed an infinite world which could be exploited further to produce ever-accelerating growth. Greens did not want this for it triggers what they viewed as undesirable features of advanced industrial societies – competitiveness, alienation, materialism and consumerism, among them. They came from many different political traditions and addressed a wide range of contemporary issues: environmental degradation, female inequality, Third World exploitation, armaments, cultural diversity, foreign workers' rights and other concerns which did not perhaps provide the essence of a coherent platform, however desirable they were.

GREEN PARTIES, PRESSURE GROUPS AND PUBLIC OPINION IN BRITAIN

For much of the last 25 years or so since the formation of the first environmentalist party in Britain, the Greens have – in the words of Pattie et al – been 'restricted to the fringes of UK politics'. 1989 provided a short-lived boost to morale, but for many supporters of the movement, pressure groups have provided more fruitful channels for their activities than political parties. The environment has not been a major dispute between the traditional parties, neither of which has taken up the cause with the seriousness and commitment demanded by many activists. In their view, politicians are willing to espouse environmental concerns when the pressure of external events or some expression of public concern makes it worthwhile, but their interest is skin-deep only.

The main parties are enthusiasts for economic growth as a means of financing their favoured projects, and in their thinking they attach great importance to the processes of industrial production and to improvements in overall living standards. They know that this is what many of their supporters want, and that however much the public may be attracted for a while to the pursuit of environment-friendly policies, in the long run many people are unwilling to sacrifice the benefits which production and materialism can provide. For instance, many people would lament the damage to the atmosphere and to small towns and villages brought about by the motor car, in the same way that they might groan about heavy traffic congestion on the roads. But when faced with the real possibility of curbs on the use of their vehicles, they quickly point to the inappropriateness of existing forms of public transport. In other words, politicians feel that the public has a lukewarm commitment to green policies, and in as much as it does embrace them, it does so with greater enthusiasm in times of prosperity than in times of recession and/or insecurity.

Such a sceptical approach by politicians places them in opposition to the goals of most ecologists. The latter believe that the pursuit of economic growth and the reluctance to challenge existing lifestyles are unsustainable policy positions, and are more prepared to place their trust in pressure-group activity than they are in the fluctuating commitment of elected representatives. This is particularly true of many younger people who despair of the possibilities of effective parliamentary action, and prefer to take direct action. In so doing, they increasingly find that they are making common cause with many other protesters who feel galvanised into action by what they see as environmental threats posed by motorway developments, the building of bypasses and the cruelty of many actions taken against animal life, among many other things.

Britain is believed to have more grass-roots direct-action environmental and social justice groups than ever before. Indeed, Vidal (*The Guardian*) reckoned that there were more than 500 separate 'actions' against authorities in the preceding year alone. Such activities reflect dissatisfaction with the decision-making process and the increasing tendency for people to resort to direct action to assert what they say are their rights, whether they are part of relatively small-scale Nimby and anti-bypass demonstrations or part of larger protests against the arms trade, opencast mining or aspects of road policy.

The greatest increase in grass-roots protest has been in city-based groups complaining against traffic congestion and pollution, including Reclaim the Streets 'parties' and the occasion when up to 8,000 protesters invaded a part of London's motorway network in July 1996. Different groups are increasingly acting in partnership, so that Justice, originally a civil rights campaigning group, is now also involved with land rights, animal rights, squatters' rights and anti-roads protests.

The linking of these direct-action groups has provided a real sense of political identity, so that Penny Kemp of the Green Party was inspired to observe (in the article quoted above) that:

> *The party politicians have got it wrong. They haven't responded to people's concerns. They've taken no notice of the new grassroots mood.*

Her party's membership has increased again of late, after the waning of earlier years. It has done so by aligning itself more to radical street politics.

Despite the falling-off from the high-point of the late 1980s and early 1990s, public support for environment groups in Britain has held up well because environmental issues have maintained wide public support even when they have not been put at the top of the political agenda. Environmental activism has generally continued to have a positive image, other than when acts of destruction have been undertaken (such as the occasional release of mink into the countryside). This may reflect the way in which popular, often local issues such as the movement of live animals or the threat to forms of wildlife, have been addressed.

In the case of the larger, more established groups, their high public profile and standing may have developed because of a perception that they have changed to a less confrontational approach. As McCormick has pointed out in relation to the national organisation of groups such as FoE and Greenpeace:

> *There has been a tendency for groups to move away from complaint and criticism and towards both research-based appeals to policy makers, industry and the public, and the provision of services and solutions.*

Thus, twin forces have been at work. On the one hand, FoE and Greenpeace have gained influence by adopting what activists often see as a more conservative stance, involving working through Whitehall, parliamentary committees, the media and Europe, whilst not forsaking the activism for which they were once condemned by 'respectable' opinion. On the other, a younger generation of activists has offered support to environmental groups, and this has sometimes resulted in a radicalisation of their attitudes and a greater willingness to engage in overtly political activities. In certain areas of public interest, established and 'respectable' groups are able and willing to campaign alongside those who use more aggressive tactics, such as Earth First! and the Earth Liberation Front.

Groups have paid more attention to influencing public attitudes in recent years. They have listened to popular demands and sought to change public behaviour via such campaigns as the attempt to change the shopping habits of consumers. The spread of information (and the consequent development of greater environmental awareness among a more educated population) has in turn meant that more pressure can be applied for policy changes on controversial topics.

As a minor party, the Greens are probably destined to lose some of their best ideas to other parties. Hence the importance of the role of pressure groups. Their task is to ensure that environmental issues are kept at the forefront of people's minds so that politicians continue to see the environment as an issue which cannot be ignored. Fervent adherents of such groups might sustain their enthusiasm in the knowledge that in one sense time is on their side, for the issues they raise are unlikely to disappear without there being action by those with the power to take the tough decisions which they believe to be necessary.

FUTURE TRENDS: OPTIMISTS AND PESSIMISTS

There are many environmental problems which continue to make demands upon those who make policy. They range from resource depletion to the provision of energy supplies, from the CAP of the EU to the problems of development in the Third World. As they confront such matters, there are different views among those sympathetic to the environmentalist case as to how the future might evolve:

- Some see the problems as being over-sold, and feel that with human ingenuity and technological advances, the problems of conservation, resource depletion and climate change can be handled. After all, the earth is a cornucopia, a paradise of plenty, and new solutions will come along to deal with existing and future problems.
- Prophets of doom maintain their dire predictions, suggesting that unless swift measures are taken, the consequences not only for humankind but for all living and non-living things are perilous. Without immediate and fundamental change, catastrophe lies ahead. They want to see a change in people's lifestyles, and believe that for individuals, the need is to cut their consumption rather than to adjust to allegedly more environmentally-friendly products.
- For many traditional politicians, the problems posed by the environment can be managed by a touch of greening here or there. Although the green diagnosis in its complete form, a form which would sacrifice economic growth, is not accepted by them, nonetheless significant progress can be made. For instance, CFCs have been removed and limits on noxious emissions can be, and have been, imposed. Bargaining and trade-offs can yield results on the environment as much as in any other sphere of political activity.

In essence, the disagreement about future scenarios is between the groups which Doyle and McEachern label the Cassandras and the Pollyannas. The Cassandras are the prophets of doom who take the view that serious environmental issues cannot be managed via existing mechanisms; for them, we are on the verge of a crisis if their message is left unheeded. They point to problems such as poverty and disease around the world, to the gap between those who have and those who have not, to the poisoning of the earth by pollutants, to the loss of diversity in nature, and to the environmental degradation associated with advanced industrialism, all set against a background of the possibility of nuclear disaster. If their position may seem unduly negative and alarmist, so that of the Pollyannas, the optimists, may seem excessively encouraging and positive. They see problems which can be managed, and warm to talk of sustainable development as the appropriate means forward for humanity.

Many members of the public might well feel unable to cope with the most dire warnings but will wish to behave responsibly. They can support green consumerism, an emphasis on better – even organic – farming and more caring treatment of animals, and they can use lead-free petrol, possibly even buy smaller cars and opt where possible for public transport. Such good deeds can all be carried out without changing their whole lifestyles or affecting the levels of economic growth.

The advantage of this kind of stance is noted by Garner, namely that:

> *it focuses on what individuals can do, thereby encouraging participation which, in turn, may lead to an increased consciousness about wider environmental issues.*

He does go on to add a note of scepticism about what is being achieved, however. He points out that some manufacturers' claims about the environmentally-friendly nature of their products are bogus or exaggerated, the example he chooses being the way in which makers of washing-up liquids used the description 'phosphate-free' for products which had never ever included phosphates anyway! Moreover, an additional difficulty with any ideas of 'shopping for a better world' as advocated by Porritt and Winner is that many of the products are more expensive or, in the case of organic foods, unattractive. They may be appealing to the concerned middle classes, but less so to those existing on a more meagre budget or those who are unwilling to compromise on the appearance of what they consume.

Yet the green cause has already made a considerable impact upon the way in which many voters think. If it did not have the same salience in the late 1990s as previously, nonetheless many members of the public and politicians have taken some of its thinking on board. They may be sceptical about the doom-laden nature of parts of the message and recoil from the recommendations of deep greens. After all, few people are likely to wish to eschew the good life which they have become accustomed to living. The more discerning and reflective, however, may be prepared to adjust their lives to incorporate a greener lifestyle and exhibit greater environmental consciousness, even if most of them are not yet ready to adopt the more fundamentalist perspective of those who see the world as heading for environmental disaster.

By now, the terminology of the green debate is familiar, and the main issues concerning the politics of the environment movement at home and abroad have been explored. This is the time to recall what you have learnt, and to develop an overview of the whole subject. For examination purposes, this is useful. Some questions invite you to take a 'broad brush' approach, requiring for instance that you 'analyse' contemporary environmental politics in Britain.

As we have seen already, it is important to look at key words. To 'analyse' is to break down complex ideas, issues and processes into component parts, and to recognise how the various parts are related. Ask yourself what are the main ideas, issues and processes relating to the politics of the environment, and perhaps make a list of them. This would be a useful exercise in helping you to respond to another type of question which is sometimes included on an examination paper:

How and why has the environment become a political issue in modern British politics?

The chart on p 116 may serve as a reminder of many of the issues dealt with in this book, and help you prepare an answer to the above question. Other material could be included of course; the chart is not intended as a definitive response.

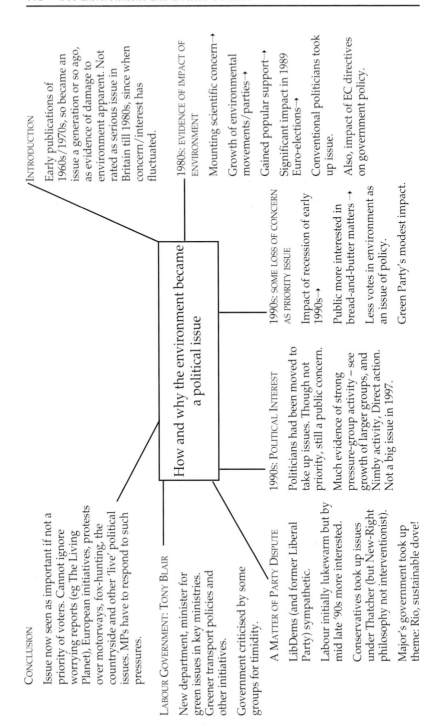

How and why the environment became a political issue

INTRODUCTION

Early publications of 1960s/1970s, so became an issue a generation or so ago, as evidence of damage to environment apparent. Not rated as serious issue in Britain till 1980s, since when concern/interest has fluctuated.

1980s: EVIDENCE OF IMPACT OF ENVIRONMENT

Mounting scientific concern→

Growth of environmental movements/parties→

Gained popular support→

Significant impact in 1989 Euro-elections→

Conventional politicians took up issue.

Also, impact of EC directives on government policy.

1990s: SOME LOSS OF CONCERN AS PRIORITY ISSUE

Impact of recession of early 1990s→

Public more interested in bread-and-butter matters →

Less votes in environment as an issue of policy.

Green Party's modest impact.

1990s: POLITICAL INTEREST

Politicians had been moved to take up issues. Though not priority, still a public concern.

Much evidence of strong pressure-group activity – see growth of larger groups, and Nimby activity, Direct action. Not a big issue in 1997.

A MATTER OF PARTY DISPUTE

LibDems (and former Liberal Party) sympathetic.

Labour initially lukewarm but by mid late '90s more interested.

Conservatives took up issues under Thatcher (but New-Right philosophy not interventionist).

Major's government took up theme: Rio, sustainable dove!

LABOUR GOVERNMENT: TONY BLAIR

New department, minister for green issues in key ministries. Greener transport policies and other initiatives.

Government criticised by some groups for timidity.

CONCLUSION

Issue now seen as important if not a priority of voters. Cannot ignore worrying reports (eg The Living Planet). European initiatives, protests over motorways, fox-hunting, the countryside and other 'live' political issues. MPs have to respond to such pressures.

FURTHER READING

There is a plethora of material on the environment, much of it covering the political aspects of the subject. However, the bulk of what has been written is inaccessible to students in sixth forms and introductory courses in Higher Education. This is in part because of the relative obscurity of some texts, making them difficult to obtain. However, accessibility is also limited by the complexity of some of the topics discussed, and more particularly by the way in which available books are written. Hence the need for a short text such as this which seeks to introduce the reader to all aspects of environmental politics.

Of the published works, *Environmental Politics* by R. Garner (1996, Prentice Hall) is probably the book most easily obtained and readily understood. Well-written, authoritative and comprehensive, it is a volume worth moving on to after a study of this more introductory guide.

Environment and Politics by T. Doyle and D. McEachern (Routledge, 1998) provides a concise analysis of key concepts and adopts a comparative approach to the study of environmental politics.

Other general works worth reading or delving into are:

Gray, T. (1995) *UK Environmental Policy in the 1990s*, Macmillan
Lowe, P. and Flynn, A. (1989) 'Environmental politics and policy in the 1980s', in
    Mohan, J. (ed.) *The Political Geography of Contemporary Britain*, Macmillan
McCormick, J. (1991) *British Politics and the Environment*, Earthscan
Young, S. (1993) *The Politics of the Environment*, Baseline Books

Environmental Groups in Politics, by P. Lowe and J. Goyder (Allen and Unwin, 1983) still provides useful insights into pressure-group activity, and its themes have been taken up and updated by W. Grant in an article in *Politics Review*, September 1995, 'Are environmental pressure groups effective?'. In the same journal, in February 1995, C. Pattie, R. Johnston and A. Russell wrote on 'The Stalled Greening of British Politics'. Again in *Politics Review*, April 1999, Robert Garner has written an early assessment of Labour's record since 1997.

Some other articles and books have been mentioned in the text, and particularly in the introduction and in the chapter on political thought, several useful ones are listed.

On specific environmental issues, FoE and Greenpeace are generous in providing introductory material, although lack of funds prevents them from dealing with more detailed enquiries.

INDEX

ACCESS TO POLITICS

Access to Politics is a series of concise and readable topic books for politics students. Each book provides advice on note-taking, tackling exam questions, developing skills of analysis, evaluation and presentation, and reading around the subject.

TITLES PUBLISHED IN 1998:

TITLES PUBLISHING IN 1999:

See page iv for information on how to order copies.